November 6–10, 2011
Denver, Colorado, USA

Association for
Computing Machinery

# SIGAda 2011

Proceedings of the 2011 ACM International Conference on

## Ada and Related Technologies

*Sponsored by:*

***ACM SIGAda***

*In cooperation with:*

***ACM SIGCSE, ACM SIGAPP, ACM SIGBED, ACM SIGPLAN, ACM SIGCAS, & Ada-Europe***

*Industrial Supporters:*

***AdaCore, Ellidiss Software, LDRA, & Rapita***

*Advancing Computing as a Science & Profession*

**The Association for Computing Machinery**
**2 Penn Plaza, Suite 701**
**New York, New York 10121-0701**



**Notice to Past Authors of ACM-Published Articles**
ACM intends to create a complete electronic archive of all articles and/or other material previously published by ACM. If you have written a work that has been previously published by ACM in any journal or conference proceedings prior to 1978, or any SIG Newsletter at any time, and you do NOT want this work to appear in the ACM Digital Library, please inform permissions@acm.org, stating the title of the work, the author(s), and where and when published.

**ISBN:** 978-1-4503-1400-8

Additional copies may be ordered prepaid from:

**ACM Order Department**
PO Box 30777
New York, NY 10087-0777, USA

Phone: 1-800-342-6626 (USA and Canada)
+1-212-626-0500 (Global)
Fax: +1-212-944-1318
E-mail: acmhelp@acm.org
Hours of Operation: 8:30 am – 4:30 pm ET

**ACM Order Number:** 825110

Printed in the USA

# Welcome to SIGAda 2011 from the Conference and Program Chairs

Welcome to the 2011 Annual International Conference of the Association for Computing Machinery's (ACM's) Special Interest Group on the Ada Programming Language (SIGAda), being held in Denver, Colorado, in the heart of the western United States.

We offer you a conference featuring a **top-quality technical program** focused on important **strengths of Ada**: safety, security, distributed, real-time, and embedded systems. The visions of these systems reflected in Ada's original requirements in the 1970s have expanded in almost unimaginable ways with the Ada 95 and Ada 2005 implementations, and continue to be objects of envy by those in the programming language community who understand what the strengths of a language bring to implementers in terms of **safety, security efficiency, reliability, and effectiveness**.

Software challenges remain dominant in these domains with rapid hardware advances. Most other languages fail to meet the needs identified as far back as the 1978 Steelman, being able at best to do only 3/4 of the needed functions, while Ada performs over 95%. Ada's track record of safety, security, reliability, efficiency, robustness and all-around success is unparalleled at solving safety/security critical, real-time and/or distributed system challenges. Ada is used in air traffic control systems, space/satellite systems, most modern jetliner avionics, high-speed ground transportation systems, and battle automation systems. As such, it is an important part of the world's economies, transportation, and defenses.

**Three days of technical papers, keynotes, and invited presentations** will report how these successes are achieved and where remaining issues are leading. We are fortunate to have **leaders in the software engineering community** to provide keynote addresses to set the tone for our conference. Beyond the formal conference of selected papers and presentations, SIGAda 2011 also offers **workshops and tutorials** with the same duality of on-theme and complementary topics. SIGAda's tutorials provide full-day or half-days on selected topics to **enhance one's professional development**. SIGAda's workshops allow those working related issues to share with each other and leverage everyone's accomplishments; workshop products are "delivered" to the community.

The broad offerings of **career-enhancing tutorials** include basic Ada language introductions for software engineers new to Ada, intermediate and advanced Ada topics for practitioners striving to expand their Ada expertise, and several language-independent technology topics. These topics are often coupled with Ada technology because only Ada's full and complete definition allows one to indicate what is expected, and to show that it can be achieved.

Join us in understanding how these topics mutually support the disciplined development and evolution of serious, high quality software systems. Finally, we hope SIGAda 2011 provides you an outstanding opportunity for **rewarding affiliation with colleagues in industry, academia, and government** — discussions "in the hall," informal meal-time meetings, and even during the more relaxed moments we make for socializing. These associations can be as valuable as the technical program at professional conferences, and often extend the experience after you return home.
We take this opportunity to thank our Corporate Sponsors. Our Platinum-level sponsor is AdaCore. Our Silver-level sponsors are Ellidiss Software, LDRA, and Rapita Systems.

ACM SIGAda Chair

Ricky E. Sward

SIGAda Program Chair

Lt Col Jeff Boleng, USAF

# Table of Contents

## Session 3: Quality and Performance



## Invited Talk

# SIGAda 2011 Conference Organization

| | |
|---|---|
| **Conference Chair:** | Ricky E. Sward *(The MITRE Corporation)* |
| **Program Chair:** | Jeff Boleng *(US Air Force Academy)* |
| **Exhibits & Sponsorships Co-Chairs:** | Greg Gicca *(AdaCore)* |
| **Proceedings Chair:** | Clyde Roby *(Institute for Defense Analyses)* |
| **Local Arrangements Co-Chairs:** | Ricky E. Sward *(The MITRE Corporation)*<br>Jeff Boleng *(US Air Force Academy)* |
| **Workshops Chair:** | Bill Thomas *(The MITRE Corporation)* |
| **Publicity Chair:** | Greg Gicca *(AdaCore)* |
| **Treasurer:** | Geoff Smith *(Lightfleet Corporation)* |
| **Registration Chair:** | Michael Feldman *(George Washington Univ., retired)* |
| **Tutorials Chair:** | Robert Pettit *(The Aerospace Corporation)* |
| **Academic Community Liaison:** | Michael Feldman *(George Washington Univ., retired)* |
| **Webmaster:** | Clyde Roby *(Institute for Defense Analyses)* |
| **SIGAda Chair:** | Ricky E. Sward *(The MITRE Corporation)* |
| **SIGAda Vice Chair for Meetings and Conferences:** | Alok Srivastava *(TASC, Inc.)* |
| **SIGAda International Representative:** | Dirk Craeynest *(K. U. Leuven, Belgium)* |
| **Program Committee:** | Jeff Boleng *(US Air Force Academy)*<br>Julien Delange *(European Space Agency)*<br>Dan Eilers *(Irvine Compiler Corporation)*<br>Michael Feldman *(George Washington Univ. retired)*<br>Mark Gardinier *(Advanced Technologies, Inc.)*<br>John Kassie *(Rockwell Collins)*<br>Sheldon Liang *(Azusa Pacific University)*<br>Karl Nyberg *(Grebyn Corporation)*<br>Jean-Pierre Rosen *(Adalog)*<br>Stephen Schwarm *(S2 Security Corporation)*<br>Frank Singhoff *(European University of Brittany)*<br>Alok Srivastava*(TASC, Inc.)*<br>Ricky Sward *(The MITRE Corporation)* |

# SIGAda 2011 Sponsors

Sponsor:

In cooperation with:

# How to Measure and Optimize Reliable Embedded Software

Dr. Ian Broster
Rapita Systems Ltd
IT Centre, York Science Park,
York YO10 5NP, UK
+44 1904 567747
ianb@rapitasystems.com

Dr. Andrew Coombes
Rapita Systems Ltd
IT Centre, York Science Park,
York YO10 5NP, UK
+44 1904 567747
acoombes@rapitasystems.com

## ABSTRACT

This tutorial explores some of the challenges of measuring performance and timing behaviour of reliable embedded systems and explains techniques and strategies for optimization of reliable software.

The tutorial explains and compares different techniques for measurement and analysis of software on embedded targets including tracing methods, in-memory analysis and using hardware support. It shows how those techniques can be used for verification of non-functional properties on-target, including in the context of DO178B/C and the new ISO26262 standard to meet the requirements for safety in automobiles.

The tutorial presents optimization at a high and low level, looking at strategies and the tradeoffs that occur in reliable software development, introducing a process that helps to ensure that optimization can have the maximum benefit for the minimum effort.

## Categories and Subject Descriptors

D.2.5 [**Testing and Debugging**]: Testing Tools– code coverage, execution time

## General Terms

Measurement, Performance, Design, Reliability, Verification.

## Keywords

Non-functional requirements, Worst-case execution time, code coverage, DO178B, ISO26262, On-target verification, Optimization.

## 1. Why do we need to optimize software?

Software timing overruns are often the root cause of intermittent failures that occur late in the project lifecycle or post deployment. When timing overruns occur, or are known to be possible, the knee-jerk response is to optimize the software: "make it faster". Unfortunately, optimizing real-time software to ensure that timing requirements are met can be both costly and time consuming.

Optimization of software is typically needed for one of two reasons. Either because it is *not* possible/practical/economic to change the hardware for a faster system, or because there are positive economic benefits to change to a cheaper (typically slower) hardware base. Such economic arguments differ widely depending on the number of units affected.


*SIGAda'11*, November 6–10, 2011, Denver, Colorado, USA.
ACM 978-1-4503-1028-4/11/11.

The decision to invest effort to optimize reliable software or not depends on a tradeoff: on the one hand there is a clear need to ensure reliable timing behaviour, but on the other we must consider the potential loss in maintainability, cost and effort to do it, cost of re-testing, cost of recertification, risk of failing to achieve the optimization goals and the impact of technical limitations such as availability of RAM and program text space.

Further, there are a number of common misconceptions and pitfalls in approaches to solving timing problems which can consume effort and resources while failing to address the underlying issues. Some of these pitfalls include: optimizing the wrong code, use of "average case" profilers, introducing new bugs and optimizing too much.

## 2. How to optimize reliable software

In this tutorial, we suggest three foundations to optimization of reliable systems software. These are: a) having good information available, b) having a managed process/strategy for managing the optimization and c) focusing on the worst case behaviour.

### 2.1 Have a process for management of optimization

Like any software project, a software optimization project benefits from having a carefully managed process. To start by writing source code is rarely the best approach.

We suggest five things to include in the project management. These are:

- Objectives: it's important to understand and state the objective of the optimization, so you can evaluate a successful project. These are also valuable to assess and "checkpoint" project progress throughout.
- Risks: understanding the risks and the mitigation strategy before you start. What are the implications of changing the source code: testing, regression errors and certification issues.
- Costs: how much effort can you afford to invest, and what is the potential return on investment?
- Planning: how will you plan the work? What does each step involve and how will it be checked?
- Evaluate: was the tradeoff worth it? Should you keep the modified code.

## 2.2 Have good information

During the technical phase of the work, key decisions need to be made on where in the application to focus attention. Ideally, a software optimization project should try to achieve maximum optimization benefit with the least effort.

A set of accurate and detailed measurements of the software executing in its target environment is essential. This is the main and most important requirement before you can begin to focus effort. Attempting to start optimization before you have this information available is risky.

For example, understanding where code appears on the longest path multiple times allows you to achieve multiple gains. Similarly, optimizing code that does not appear on the worst case path is not only wasting time, but risking introducing regression bugs needlessly.

There are a number of challenges that arise in assessing executable qualities through on-target measurement. Tool support is invaluable in this area, however. There are several issues to address:

1. Level of detail. Coarse timing measurements are insufficient to many optimization strategies. Often the execution time of code (especially in languages such as Ada) is unrelated to the number of lines of code. Hidden code (such as array copies, initialization and finalization) are frequently observed to be causes of unexpected execution time that can be easily optimized out of code. Collecting measurements in detail (such as down to block level) is a power tool for finding potential optimization candidates.
2. Effort of process. A manual process of performing measurements is slow and error prone. An automatic tool to repeat measurements is important. Our experience is that with bigger/more complex the systems, the effort required to obtain accurate data manually increases quickly to beyond practical capabilities.
3. Method for extracting information. The mechanism for measuring needs to be fairly non-intrusive, accurate and reliable. A key challenge with on-target verification is the influence that the act of measurement itself can have on the results obtained. This is referred to as the probe effect. For example, adding instrumentation points to the source code changes the code size, execution time, and may also increase stack usage.
4. Adequate test coverage. Clearly, to have confidence in the measurements that are taken, the code must be adequately tested. One way to ensure adequate testing is to use structural code coverage metrics, such as statement coverage, or even MC/DC coverage. Tool support such as RapiCover [1] can help to provide confidence in testing strategy.

Measurement of software running on-target presents significant technical challenges, some of which can be overcome with tool support, innovative use of spare RAM, I/O and buses.

## 2.3 Focus on worst case behavior

In the design of reliable systems, we are familiar with looking at the worst case scenario and analyzing what might happen. The same mentality is vital in a software optimization project.

A common error in software optimization is to attempt to optimize the "average case" behaviour. For example, adding ways to exit early from loops, or to provide some level of data caching. These techniques are good and standard ways to improve the average case.

However, in reliable systems development, we are concerned with ensuring that the software *always* finishes on time with predictable, reliable behaviour. Reducing the average case does not automatically support this goal.

Furthermore, average case optimizations are frequently observed to make the worst case even worse and therefore increase the risk/frequency of timing overruns. For example, consider adding an early exit from a loop – the worst case is that we still have to execute every iteration, but now there is an extra test in every iteration of the loop.

Finally, one of the risks of using a profiler is that you optimize the wrong code altogether. A profiler (also called a sampling profiler) reports where the program execution spends most of its time – i.e. it reports the average case path. However, we must focus on the worst case scenario, which may only happen infrequently, and therefore may be completely unnoticed by a profiler. The worst case path might include error cases, or be triggered by maximal or unusual input data. Tools such as RapiTime [1], which focus on the worst case path help to avoid this by highlighting code that appears on the worst case path.

# 3. Case Study

An example leading to the work presented in this tutorial includes work on the BAE Systems' Hawk Mission Computer. The objective was to reduce the overall worst case execution time of the Mission Computer operational Flight Program by 10%, in order to generate headroom to add new functionality without the need for costly hardware upgrades.

The software was written in Ada and was over 100K LOC in 25 scheduled partitions.

The RapiTime timing analysis tool was used to analyze four partitions in detail. The tool allowed accurate and detailed measurements to be taken using a lightweight tracing technique. The worst case execution time (WCET) was analyzed and three of optimization candidates that appeared on the worst case path were selected for review.

The optimization candidates were: a) redundant copies of large data structures could be removed, b) heavy use of bit-packing code in Ada could be optimized using assembler c) conditionals called frequently on the worst case path could be replaced with a look up table.

The optimizations, when applied achieved a 23% reduction in the worst case execution time. The effort taken was estimated to be around 10% of the effort required to perform the work without tool support.

# 4. ACKNOWLEDGMENTS

The research leading to these results has received funding from the European Community's Seventh Framework Programme (FP7/2007-2013) under grant agreement n° 249100.

# 5. REFERENCES

[1] RVS (Rapita Verification Suite). RapiTime WCET and Timing Analysis and RapiCover structural coverage tool. http://www.rapitasystems.com/

Tutorial

# Service-Oriented Architecture (SOA) Concepts and Implementations

Ricky E. Sward
The MITRE Corporation
1155 Academy Park Loop
Colorado Springs, CO 80910
rsward@mitre.org

Jeff Boleng
US Air Force Academy
2354 Fairchild Drive
USAF Academy, CO 80840
jeff.boleng@usafa.edu

## Abstract

This tutorial explains how to implement a Service-Oriented Architecture (SOA) for reliable systems using Enterprise Service Bus (ESB) technologies. The first half of the tutorial describes terms of Service-Oriented Architectures (SOA) including service, service registry, service provider, service consumer, Simple Object Access Protocol (SOAP), Representational State Transfer (REST), and Web Service Description Language (WSDL). Several examples of REST and SOAP web services are provided using the Ada Web Server (AWS). This tutorial also presents principles of SOA including loose coupling, encapsulation, composibility of web services, and statelessness of web services. The tutorial covers the benefits of SOA and organizations that are supporting SOA infrastructure. The second half of the tutorial covers Enterprise Service Bus (ESB) technologies including definitions, capabilities, benefits and drawbacks. The tutorial discusses the difference between SOA and an ESB, as well as some of the commercially available ESB solutions on the market. The Mule ESB is explored in more detail and several examples are given. Several examples of using an ESB in a SOA application are given using AWS as an Ada implementation. An AWS server is built in the examples and connected to the ESB providing REST and SOAP web services. AWS allows the developer to expose services in a high-integrity system using the Ada and SPARK programming languages. This tutorial is slightly different than the one given at Ada Europe 2008 in that it will focus more on the application of SOA and ESB technology to reliable, high-integrity systems. All tutorial material will be provided to attendees and the opportunity for hands-on participation in examples will be possible.

**Categories & Subject Descriptors:** D.2 Software Engineering, D.3 Programming Languages

**General Terms:** Algorithms, Design, Languages.


*SIGAda'11*, November 6–10, 2011, Denver, Colorado, USA.
ACM 978-1-4503-1028-4/11/11.

## Bio

Ricky E. "Ranger" Sward is a Lead Information Systems Engineer for the MITRE Corporation in Colorado Springs, CO, USA. He currently supports the Air Force A2U Unmanned Systems ISR Innovations branch working to integrate full-motion video initiatives for unmanned aircraft systems. Ranger retired from the Air Force in August 2006 after a 21 year career as a Communications and Computer officer. He taught at the US Air Force Academy for 10 years where he taught courses such as Software Engineering and Unmanned Aircraft Systems. He has a B.S. and an M.S. in Computer Science, as well as a Ph.D. in Computer Engineering.

LtCol Jeff Boleng is an Associate Professor of Computer Science at the USAF Academy in Colorado Springs, CO, USA. He teaches a wide variety of computer science courses in programming, computer security, networking, operating systems, and algorithms. His operational Air Force Experience includes evaluating and implementing SOA solutions for command and control and knowledge management applications. He is a 1991 graduate of the US Air Force Academy and has an M.S. (1997) and Ph.D. (2002) in Mathematical and Computer Sciences from Colorado School of Mines.

Tutorial

# DO-178C: The Next Avionics Safety Standard

Benjamin M. Brosgol
AdaCore
New York, NY, USA
brosgol@adacore.com

## Abstract

The commercial avionics community's DO-178B software safety certification requirements document is being updated to take into account twenty years of experience, and the new version (DO-178C) is close to completion. This half-day tutorial covers the core of the DO-178C standard, including the new treatment of tool qualification, as well the supplements on Object-Oriented and Other Technologies, Model-Based Design, and Formal Methods.

**Categories & Subject Descriptors:** D.2 SOFTWARE ENGINEERING (K.6.3)

**General Terms:** Design, Reliability, Security, Standardization, Languages, Verification.

**Keywords:** Safety certification, DO-178B, DO-178C, Object-Oriented Technologies

## Bio

Dr. Benjamin Brosgol is a senior member of the technical staff of AdaCore. He has been involved with programming language design and implementation for more than 30 years, concentrating on languages and technologies for high-integrity systems. Dr. Brosgol was a member of the design team for Ada 95, and he has also served in the Expert Groups for several Java Specification Requests. He has presented papers and tutorials on safety and security certification on numerous occasions including ESC (Embedded Systems Conference), ICSE (IEEE/ACM International Conference on Software Engineering), SSTC (Systems & Software Technology Conference), ACM SIGAda, and Ada-Europe. Dr. Brosgol is a former Chair of ACM SIGAda. He holds a BA in Mathematics from Amherst College, and MS and PhD degrees in Applied Mathematics from Harvard University.


*SIGAda'11*, November 6–10, 2011, Denver, Colorado, USA.
ACM 978-1-4503-1028-4/11/11.

# Improving Quality of Ada Software with Range Analysis


Jay Abraham
MathWorks
3 Apple Hill Drive
Natick, MA 01760, USA
1 (508) 647-3027
jabraham@mathworks.com

Jeff Chapple
MathWorks
3 Apple Hill Drive
Natick, MA 01760, USA
1 (508) 647-8045
jchapple@mathworks.com

Cyril Preve
MathWorks
100 C alle Saint-Exupery
Montbonnot 38330, France
33-4-56-80-6731
cpreve@mathworks.com



## ABSTRACT

Ada is a strong language with built-in mechanisms that naturally lead to less risky software programs. This is possible because Ada is a structured and strongly typed language with built-in run-time protection mechanisms. For example, subtyping allows for specification of ranges for variable. The compiler can detect illegal values for these variables as well as insert run-time range checks during compilation so that violating specified ranges result in a Constraint_Error during run-time.

For complex embedded systems where quality and reliabiity are imperative, the Ada programming language alone may not provide sufficient quality margins. Demonstrating run-time robustness with exhaustive dynamic testing is not possible. Formal methods with mathematical proofs enables precise determination of some properties of a complex system without the need for exhaustive analysis. This technique can be exploited statically to exhaustively determine dynamic runtime behavior of software programs.

Coupling the Ada language with these state of the art verification solutions may improve the predictability of quality and safety. This tutorial examines software verification and testing approaches that have been applied to Ada programs. These techniques will be compared and contrasted with formal methods based techniques that can statically produce accurate variable range analysis of Ada programs. Concrete technical examples will be explored to see how these verification techniques, in particular the use of range analysis, can be used to improve the quality and safety of complex software systems that are developed in Ada.



## Categories and Subject Descriptors

D.2.4 [**Software**]: Software / Program Verification – *correctness proofs, formal methods, reliability, validation.*

## General Terms

Reliability, Verification.

## Keywords

Static code analysis, abstract interpretation, code verification, variable range analysis, software quality assurance.




*SIGAda'11,* November 6–10, 2011, Denver, Colorado, USA.
ACM 978-1-4503-1028-4/11/11.


## 1. Tutorial Agenda

This tutorial will span approximately three hours. Presentations will be interspersed with live demonstrations showing how Ada software can fail with run-time errors and how these errors can be detected and debugged. Formal methods based techniques to achieve runtime verification and role of range analysis will be discussed. Slices of Ada source code will be analyzed from a runtime verification perspective to gauge the effectiveness of this technique. The role of range analysis for Ada programs will be shown with examples. Questions and interaction with the audience will be highly encouraged. The detailed agenda is provided below.

1. Considerations for Risk and Safety when Programming in Ada
   a. Even though Ada is a safe language, run-time errors can still occur
   b. Examples of famous software failures due to run-time errors
2. Use of Ada in Critical Systems
   a. Overview of the use of Ada in various critical systems
3. Improving the Quality of Programs Written in the Ada Language
   a. Discuss various methods of review and test
   b. Can software programs be exhaustively tested or verified?
4. Formal Methods Techniques and Their Application
   a. Overview of formal methods
   b. Introduce Abstract Interpretation as a formal methods technique
   c. Coupling formal methods with static analysis
   d. Using these techniques to produce accurate variable ranges in Ada
5. Tools that Perform Variable Range Analysis
   a. Overview of academic and commercial tools
6. Using Range Analysis to Improve Software Quality
   a. Source code examples
   b. Highlight finding and debugging defects with range analysis
7. The vision of zero defect software
   a. Is this possible?
   b. Getting nearer to the goal of zero defect software
8. Conclusion

Tutorial

# SF1: Introduction to Ada

Michael B. Feldman
The George Washington University (retired)
Washington, DC USA
Mfeldman@GWU.Edu

## Abstract

Level – Beginner, but attendees should have some experience with a high-level programming language.

This tutorial is designed for those who have some familiarity with a programming language, but who are new to Ada. In the morning, we will discuss the basics of programming in Ada, including types, packages, syntax rules, and other Ada programming constructs. In the afternoon, we will briefly cover Ada's object-oriented programming and concurrent-programming features. Many examples will be shown; freely downloadable Ada programming environments and tools will be discussed.

**Categories & Subject Descriptors:** D.2 Software Engineering, D.3 Programming Languages

**General Terms:** Algorithms, Design, Documentation, Languages, Standardization.

## Bio

Michael B. Feldman received the B.S.E. degree in Electrical Engineering from Princeton University, and the M.S. and Ph.D. degrees in Computer and Information Sciences from the University of Pennsylvania.

In 1975, Dr. Feldman joined the Computer Science faculty at The George Washington University, from which he retired in 2007 as Professor Emeritus. He now resides in Portland, Oregon.

While at GW, he taught a large number of different courses, from freshman to doctoral level. For many years he was responsible for the CS majors oriented introductory programming course, and the undergraduate data structures and real-time systems courses. He received the Computer Science Professor of the Year Award in 2002, 2003, and 2006, and the University's Oscar and Shoshana Trachtenberg Teaching Prize in 2003. From 1999 to 2005, he served as chairman of the Computer Science Curriculum Committee.

Dr. Feldman is the author of *Ada 95: Problem Solving and Program Design,* and *Software Construction and Data Structures with Ada 95,* which have been among the best-selling texts of their kind. The latter book's Ada 83 edition, published in 1985, was the first Ada- related text specifically targeted to undergraduate courses. Dr. Feldman also wrote "Ada 95 in Context" -- the Ada chapter in Macmillan's *Handbook of Programming Languages* -- as well as the Software Engineering Institute Curriculum Module CM-25, "Language and System Support for Concurrent Programming," and "Inspiring Our Undergraduate Students' Aspirations," published in the quarterly of the ACM Special Interest Group on Computer Science Education.


*SIGAda '11*, November 6–10, 2011, Denver, Colorado, USA.
ACM 978-1-4503-1028-4/11/11.

# Tutorial: Experimenting with ParaSail – Parallel Specification and Implementation Language

S. Tucker Taft
SofCheck, Inc.
11 Cypress Drive
Burlington, MA 01803 USA
+1-781-750-8068
tucker.taft@sofcheck.com

## ABSTRACT

This tutorial provides an opportunity to experiment with a new language designed to support the safe, secure, and productive development of parallel programs. ParaSail is a new language with pervasive parallelism coupled with extensive compile-time checking of annotations in the form of assertions, preconditions, postconditions, etc. ParaSail does all checking at compile time, and eliminates race conditions, null dereferences, uninitialized data access, numeric overflow, out of bounds indexing, etc. as well as statically checking the truth of all user-written assertions. After a short introduction to the language, attendees will receive a prototype ParaSail compiler and an accompanying ParaSail Virtual Machine interpreter for writing and testing ParaSail programs. The tutorial/workshop will finish with a group discussion and feedback on the experience of using this new language.

## Categories and Subject Descriptors

D.2.4 [**Software Engineering**]: Software/Program Verification – *formal methods, programming by contract*; D.3.3 [**Programming Languages**]: Language Contructs and Features – *abstract data types, concurrent programming structures, dynamic storage management, polymorphism.*

## General Terms

Algorithms, Reliability, Languages, Theory, Verification.

## Keywords

ParaSail, Parallel Programming, Formal Methods, Pointer-free Programming, Expandable Objects

## 1. DESCRIPTION

This tutorial/workshop will provide a chance to experiment with a new language designed to support the safe, secure, and productive development of parallel programs. ParaSail is a new language targeted at safety-critical and high-security systems development in a "multi-core" world, with pervasive parallelism coupled with extensive compile-time checking of annotations in the form of assertions, preconditions, postconditions, etc[1]. ParaSail does all checking at compile time by incorporating an advanced static analysis engine, allowing it to eliminate race conditions, null dereferences, uninitialized data access, numeric overflow, out of bounds indexing, etc. as well as statically checking the truth of all user-written assertions.

The tutorial/workshop will begin with a short introduction to the language,. After that, the attendees will receive a prototype ParaSail compiler and an accompanying ParaSail Virtual Machine interpreter for writing and testing ParaSail programs. A set of sample programs will be provided as a starting point for experimentation. The tutorial/workshop will finish with a group discussion and feedback on the experience of using this new language, and ideas about next steps.

## 2. Outline

I. Introduction to ParaSail
   a. Goals of Language
   b. Overall Model of Modules, Types, Objects and Operations
   c. Parallelism Features
   d. Annotation Features

II. ParaSail Compiler and Virtual Machine
   a. Sample program demonstrations of compiler and VM
   b. Time for attendees to modify sample programs or write new ones
   c. Time for compiling and testing the attendee programs

III. Group discussion and feedback session
   a. Demos of attendee-written programs
   b. Reactions to the new language
   c. Suggestions for improvements
   d. Discussion of possible next steps

## 3. Level

The tutorial includes an introduction to the language. No specific prerequisites other than an interest and ability in learning a new language, plus a basic understanding of parallelism, assertions, preconditions, and postconditions.

## 4. Reasons for attending

This is a chance to experiment with a new programming language oriented around parallelism and formal verification. The language is still in development, so it is also a chance to help


*SIGAda'11,* November 6–10, 2011, Denver, Colorado, USA.
ACM 978-1-4503-1028-4/11/11.

improve and refine the language, and perhaps gain some insights that might contribute to other language design efforts.

## 5. Short Biography

The presenter has been involved with language design since 1975, and with Ada since 1980. He was the technical lead for the design of Ada 95, and was heavily involved in the design of Ada 2005 and the ongoing design of Ada 2012. In addition to language design, the presenter has been the technical lead on the development of an Ada 83 and of an Ada 95 compiler, as well as of an advanced language-independent static analysis technology

## 6. REFERENCES


[1] Taft, S. Tucker. 2011 Blog: Designing ParaSail, a new programming language. http://parasail-programming-language.blogspot.com.

SIGAda'11 Tutorial Summary

# Designing and Checking Coding Standards for Ada

Jean-Pierre Rosen
Adalog
Issy-Les-Moulineaux, France
rosen@adalog.fr

## Abstract

Most companies have developed coding standards (often because having one is a requirement for certification), but few have conducted a real analysis of the value, consistency, and efficiency of the coding standard.

This tutorial presents the challenges of establishing a coding standard, not just for the sake of having one, but with the goal of actually improving the quality of software. This implies not only having "good" rules, but also having rules that are understood, accepted, and adhered to by the programming team.

The issues of automatically checking the rules is also fundamental: experience shows that no manual checking can cover the programming rules to a satisfactory extent. The tutorial presents the tools available, then goes into deeper details using AdaControl, a free rules checking tool.

Attendees are invited to bring their own code and computers, for practical experiment of how automatic checking can help discover violations that have escaped the most thorough reviews.

**Categories & Subject Descriptors:** D.2.3 [SOFTWARE ENGINEERING]: Coding Tools and Techniques – *Standards*.

**General Terms:** Verification.

## Bio

JP Rosen is a professional teacher, teaching Ada (since 1979, it was preliminary Ada!), methods, and software engineering. He runs Adalog, a company specialized in providing training, consultancy, and services in all areas connected to the Ada language and software engineering. He is chairman of AFNOR's (French standardization body) Ada group, AFNOR's spokeperson at WG9, member of the Vulnerabilities group of WG9, and chairman of Ada-France.

Adalog offers regularly on-site and off-site training sessions in Ada. Adalog has developed AdaControl, a free popular coding standard checking tool, and has helped several customers in devising their own coding standard.


*SIGAda'11*, November 6–10, 2011, Denver, Colorado, USA.
ACM 978-1-4503-1028-4/11/11.

# Building Embedded Real-Time Applications

John McCormick
University of Northern Iowa
mccormick@cs.uni.edu

Frank Singhoff
Université de Bretagne Occidentale
singhoff@univ-brest.fr

## Abstract

The arrival and popularity of multi-core processors has sparked a renewed interest in the development of parallel programs. Similarly, the availability of low cost microprocessors and sensors has generated a great interest in embedded real-time programs. Ada is arguably the most appropriate language for development of parallel and real-time applications. This tutorial provides an introduction to the features of Ada that makes it appropriate in these domains including:

- The Ada type model
- High level support for low level programming
- The task
- Communication and synchronization based on shared objects
- Communication and synchronization based on direct interaction
- Real-time systems and scheduling concepts
- Real-Time programming with Ada

We encourage tutorial participants to bring a laptop on which they can install Cheddar for hands on exercises.

**Categories & Subject Descriptors:** C.3 [Special-Purpose And Application-Based Systems]: Real-time and embedded systems, D.1.3 [Programming Techniques]: Concurrent Programming – *parallel programming*, D.3.3 [Programming Languages]: Language Constructs and Features – *concurrent programming structures*, J.7 [Computers in other Systems]: Real time.

**General Terms:** Performance, Design, Languages.

## Bios

John McCormick is Professor of Computer Science at the University of Northern Iowa. He began his career in computer science at the State University of New York in 1979. In 1993 John was awarded the *Chancellor's Award for Excellence in Teaching*. He has served as Secretary, Treasurer, and Chair of ACM SIGAda. He received the *SIGAda Distinguished Service Award* in 2002 and the *SIGAda Outstanding Ada Community Contributions Award* in 2008. He was awarded the *SIGAda Best Paper and Presentation Award* in 1991 and the *Ada Europe Best Presentation Award* in 2008.

Frank Singhoff is Professor of Computer Science and head of the Computer Science Department at the Université de Bretagne Occidentale, France. He received his engineering degree in Computer Science from the CNAM/Paris in 1996 and his PhD from Télécom-Paris-Tech in 1999. Frank Singhoff is part of the LISyC laboratory. His current research focuses on real-time scheduling theory and architecture description languages. His research work has led to the development of an open-source toolset called Cheddar, a toolset designed to perform analysis with the real-time scheduling theory. Frank Singhoff is also member of the AADL/AS-2C committee of the SAE. He received the *SIGAda Outstanding Ada Community Contributions Award* in 2010.


*SIGAda'11*, November 6–10, 2011, Denver, Colorado, USA.
ACM 978-1-4503-1028-4/11/11.

# Everything I Know I Learned From Ada

Grady Booch
IBM Research
egrady@booch.com

## ABSTRACT

I entered the world of Ada at a most impressionable time in my career: I knew enough to be dangerous, but not so much that I was unwilling to try new things. Ada was full of new things that have informed much of what I do today. The role of abstraction, the meaning of beauty in design, the nature of delivering ultra-large software-intensive systems, collaboration across geographic and cultural boundaries, the joys and frustrations of standards building, the process of revolution: these are all things I have learned from Ada. In this presentation, I'll offer some war stories from the past and offer speculation on the future.

## Categories and Subject Descriptors

D.3.0 Programming Languages, General D.2.0 Software engineering, General

## General Terms

Design, Standardization, Languages.

## Keywords

Software engineering, programming languages, object-oriented analysis and design, peopleware, methodology.


*SIGAda '11*, November 6–10, 2011, Denver, Colorado, USA.
ACM 978-1-4503-1028-4/11/11.

# A Parallel Programming Model for Ada

Hazem Ali
CISTER Research Centre
Polytechnic Institute of Porto, Portugal
haali@isep.ipp.pt

Luís Miguel Pinho
CISTER Research Centre
Polytechnic Institute of Porto, Portugal
lmp@isep.ipp.pt

## ABSTRACT

Over the last three decades, computer architects have been able to achieve an increase in performance for single processors by, e.g., increasing clock speed, introducing cache memories and using instruction level parallelism. However, because of power consumption and heat dissipation constraints, this trend is going to cease. In recent times, hardware engineers have instead moved to new chip architectures with multiple processor cores on a single chip. With multi-core processors, applications can complete more total work than with one core alone.

To take advantage of multi-core processors, parallel programming models are proposed as promising solutions for more effectively using multi-core processors. This paper discusses some of the existent models and frameworks for parallel programming, leading to outline a draft parallel programming model for Ada.

## Categories and Subject Descriptors

D.3.3 [**Programming Languages**]: Language Contructs and Features – *Concurrent programming structures, Ada.* D.1.3 [**Programming Techniques**]: Concurrent Programming – *Parallel Programming.*

## General Terms

Design, Standardization, Languages.

## Keywords

Ada, Many-core systems, Parallel programming, Lightweight threads model

## 1. INTRODUCTION

Multi-core architectures, integrating several processors on a single chip, are quickly becoming widespread, even in small embedded systems. This cheaply available computational power makes parallel programming more than ever a concern for software developers, since the sequential programming model does not scale well for such multi-core systems [1].

The current trend to use multi-core platforms will thus not provide improvements on the performance of software, and may even impact its reliability, if programming environments are not also evolved to account for the new paradigm of naturally parallel hardware [2]. It is recognized that new (or old) parallel programming models are needed to take advantage of (large) parallel platforms, that data structures, algorithms and code generation tools must be made aware of the underlying architecture changes, and that programming should be independent of the number of processors, to shield from likely hardware evolution. The problem is exacerbated for platforms with larger number of cores (usually noted as many-core).

It is not a surprise that many research projects and commercial frameworks have been either proposing new or re-using old models, specifically targeting the potentially large-scale parallelism found in multi-cores. Frameworks such as Cilk [3], Intel's Threading Building Blocks [4], Java Fork/Join [5], OpenMP [6], Microsoft's Task Parallel Library [7], StackThreads/MP [8] or Paraffin [9] provide a model where the programmer divides the application in numerous potentially parallel computing units[1], which are then dynamically assigned to worker threads in the cores by the frameworks' runtime, considering the actual load in the system. To deal with the load balancing of these parallel units in the worker threads (and thus in the cores), the work-stealing algorithm [10] is currently one of the most widely-used, although it may not perform better in all cases [11].

Work-stealing has the advantage of reducing task contention, due to the support for double-ended queues, with LIFO behaviour when worker-threads process their own-generated units, and FIFO behaviour when threads steal from other threads queues. Another advantage is that as soon as one unit migrates (is stolen) to a new core, all units generated by it are placed in this core queue, thus decreasing the need for further stealing. Finally, as threads execute units in LIFO order, they maximize the probability of data still being in the cache. Contrarily, stealing is performed in the other end of the queue, targeting older units, minimizing the probability of the data being in the cache (of the old wrong core).

This parallel programming model based on potentially parallel computation units also provides higher-abstraction advantages. For instance, the programmer can focus on writing functional code, only explicitly specifying potentially parallel operations, leaving to the underlying framework the dynamic mapping of units to threads. This separation of concerns leads to more reliable code, and more optimized runtimes. Also, it improves programmer productivity.



[1] These units may be called lightweight threads, tasks, pJobs, depending on the context and framework. For consistency and simplicity in this paper (and to not clash with the Ada notion of task) we use potentially parallel computation units.

Also, the composability of several different components, all using this model is easily performed, as these components only create the units, being all of them scheduled by the underlying runtime.

Obviously, this approach introduces some overhead, both on data structures needed to manage the computation units and their mapping to cores, but also on the migration of units (and eventual impact in caches). However, it is important to note that stealing only takes place if a particular core is idle. Therefore, the overhead is not significant, particularly as the number of cores increases larger than the number of concurrent activities (threads) of an application.

Considering the above, it is important to assess the use of this model in Ada. Although multi-core programming support will be available in the forthcoming revision of the language (Ada 2012) [12], the programming model of Ada will still be based on the definition of heavier task units, as it is targeted to environments where the number of cores is far less than the number of application tasks.

The structure of the paper is as follows. The next section reviews some previous attempts to define parallelism in Ada. Section 3 then provides an overview of several current parallel programming models using potentially parallel computation units. Afterwards, Section 4 provides and discusses the proposed Ada model. Finally, some conclusions are presented.

## 2. PARALLEL PROGRAMMING AND ADA

It is important to note that parallel programming approaches in Ada were considered several years ago (e.g. [13,14,15]) [2]. The work in [13] introduces a `parallel` keyword, for `for loops`, allowing a specific compiler to optimize loop iterations, targeted to a multiprocessor platform. The work in [14] is similar, as it also targets the optimization of parallel loops; furthermore, the authors state that Ada tasks are not the appropriate unit of parallelization thus proposing a concept of minitasks which can be optimized by compilers and runtimes aware of this model. It is interesting to note that [14] already puts forward some of the ideas that are currently being (again) discussed concerning the use of tasks/threads for manycores, in particular the excessive context and initiation overhead which is required to manage tasks in parallel machines. The solution proposed is in line with the current move to provide more efficient parallel units.

Contrarily, in [15] the author proposed a model for integrating parallel dataflow programming with the Ada tasking model, proposing two extension keywords to standard Ada: `parallel` and `single`. The `parallel` keyword is used for declaring explicitly that a set (block) of statements or a `for loop` will be executed in parallel. It transforms these into a sequence of task declarations with a separate task representing each statement or iteration respectively. On the other hand, the `single` keyword is used for declaring single-assignment types (also known as immutables) for exchanging data and synchronization between parallel blocks.

After that, the research evolved in [16] by defining a new programming language called Declarative Ada where parallelism is implicit. Declarative Ada is a programming language based on a Pascal-like subset of Ada. The difference between Declarative Ada and the previously proposed extension is that all variables are considered as single-assignment. This allows implicit parallel execution of programs with synchronization through run-time dataflow.

Although in Declarative Ada all statements can be executed in parallel, we believe that it will not be up to the expectations from the point of view of performance. This comes from the fact that all parallel executions are mapped to Ada tasks, thus creating higher overhead during execution that will eliminate any gained speedup from parallel execution [14] Moreover, this very fine grain parallelism, which comes from the fact that each statement is a parallel block, may lead to a mass synchronization overhead between different parallel blocks. This means degraded overall performance.

The previous discussion demonstrate the growing need for constructs or methods that define true parallelism in Ada away from the well known task model, which should be used for concurrency. As Robert Harper states: *"The first thing to understand is parallelism has nothing to do with concurrency"* [17]. Parallelism is concerned with efficiency of programs operating in parallel platforms, and where the output results are deterministic.

Concurrency, on the other hand, refers to the nondeterministic execution of applications where expected and unexpected events must me managed. Such situations are not concerned with efficiency and performance as much as getting the system to operate correctly and under control. Concurrent systems can be implemented in parallel platforms, but can also be in sequential ones.

The task model of Ada is undoubtedly suitable for concurrent systems, where each task maps to an application concurrent activity, that can abort, suspend or resume its execution according to the system requirements. Orthogonal to this model, parallel constructs proposed for Ada should adopt a lightweight model, i.e., lightweight computation units used as building blocks, mapped to a pool of worker (system) tasks/threads with a special purpose scheduling discipline.

This is the model of a more recent approach to provide parallel programming support in Ada [9], with support to potential parallel computation units, with work-sharing, work-seeking and work-stealing functionality through an external library. Our proposal, although in the same context, is different, proposing that Ada revisits its parallel programming model, intending to explore a language based approach that hides from the programmer the concrete mapping of the application into the parallel platform whilst allowing him/her to define the potentially parallel blocks.

## 3. PARALLEL PROGRAMMING MODELS

In order to propose a parallel programming model for Ada, it is important to analyze currently used approaches for the design of parallel programs. In the brief analysis in this paper, the common example of the Fibonacci function will be used to present the most relevant features of each approach. Note that although the iterative version of the Fibonacci function is more efficient than the recursive version, the recursive version may be a better solution in parallel platforms, when a large percentage of the time processors are idle. Furthermore, it is a good example of a simply parallelizable function.

[2] There is indeed a general trend to look back to the past in all areas of computers as parallel platforms become widespread.

The first example we present is how to develop the function by using Ada tasks as the unit of parallelization. Two approaches are shown. The first approach (Listing 1) creates one task per function execution, in order to potentially (and naively) try to maximize parallelism. It is clear that the overhead of task creation will impair the advantages of the parallelization.

```
task type Fib (N: Natural) is
   entry Result(R: out Natural);
end Fib;
task body Fib is
   Res, N1, N2: Natural;
   Fib_Acc_N1, Fib_Acc_N2 : access Fib;
begin
   if Value < 2 then
      Res := Value;
   else
      Fib_Acc_N1 := new Fib(N - 1);
      Fib_Acc_N2 := new Fib(N - 2);
      Fib_Acc_N1.Result(N1);
      Fib_Acc_N2.Result(N2);
      Res := N1 + N2;
   end if;
   accept Result(R: out Natural) do
      R := Res;
   end Result;
end Fib;
```

**Listing 1 – Fibonacci Example #1**

The second (naïve) example (Listing 2) uses the number of cores information to divide the problem, thus creating one task per core. The program gets more complex as it is necessary to consider the relation between the number of cores and the size of the problem, and it is necessary to keep track of the available tasks. If a task is not available, then the calculation will be done with a sequential version of the algorithm.

Note that the size of the problem will not be the same on each core, thus there will be idle cores while other will be overloaded. If the programmer attempts to do a load balancing solution, he/she will end up with redeveloping a complete work-sharing or work-stealing algorithm.

```
function Seq_Fib (N : in Natural)
      return Natural is
begin
   if Value < 2 then
      return N;
   return Seq_Fib (N - 1) +
          Seq_Fib (N - 2);
end Seq_Fib;
```

```
task type Fib is
   entry Value (N: in Natural);
   entry Result(R: out Natural);
end Fib;

protected Task_Pool is
   procedure Try_Get(T: out access Fib;
                     Val: Natural);
private
   Workers: array (1..CPU_Count) of Fib;
end Task_Pool;

task body Fib is
  Val, N1, N2: Natural;
  Fib_Acc_N1, Fib_Acc_N2 : access Fib;
begin
   loop
      accept Value (N: in Natural) do
         Val := N;
      end Value;
      if Value < 2 then
          Res := Value;
      else
         -- try parallel of both branches
         Task_Pool.Try_Get(Fib_Acc_N1,
                           Val - 1);
         Task_Pool.Try_Get(Fib_Acc_N2,
                           Val - 2);
         if Fib_Acc_N1 /= null then
            Fib_Acc_N1.Result(N1);
         else
            N1 := Seq_Fib (Val - 1);
         end if;
         if Fib_Acc_N2 /= null then
            Fib_Acc_N2.Result(N2);
         else
            N2 := Seq_Fib (Val - 2);
         end if;
      end if;
      accept Result(R: out Natural) do
         R := N1 + N2;
      end Result;
```

```
      end loop;
   end Fib;
   protected Task_Pool is
      procedure Try_Get(T: out access Fib;
                        Val: Natural) is
      begin
         for I in 1..CPU_Count loop
            select
               Workers(I).Value(Val);
               T := Workers(I)'access;
               exit;
            else
               null;
            end select;
            T := null;
         end loop;
      end Try_Get;
   end Task_Pool;
```

**Listing 2 – Fibonacci Example #2**

The next sub sections present three different frameworks, all based on creating potentially parallel computation units, following the technique described in the Introduction. These frameworks are different, as they follow different approaches: a library based one; a pre-processor based one, and a language based one.

## 3.1 Library-based approaches

The example of a library-based approach is provided using the Intel's Threading Building Blocks [4], which is a library, implemented using the C++ Standard Template Library, and that provides the required classes to design and manage the parallel computation units, called tasks.

```
class FibTask: public task {
public:
   const long n; long* const sum;
   FibTask( long n_, long* sum_)
       : n(n_), sum(sum_) {}

   task* execute() {
      if(n < 2) {
         *sum = n;
      } else {
         long x, y;
         FibTask& a =
            *new(allocate_child())
             FibTask(n-1,&x);
         FibTask& b =
            *new(allocate_child())
             FibTask(n-2,&y);
         set_ref_count(3);
         spawn( b );
         spawn_and_wait_for_all( a );
         *sum = x+y;
      }
      return NULL;
   }
}
```

**Listing 3 – TBB Example**

This code in Listing 3 uses an object of the class `FibTask`, which inherits from the special class task, to do the actual work. It starts by creating two new task objects to compute `n-1` and `n-2`, and then spawns these tasks (the last one is a spawn and wait which will cause the main task to wait for the two children). Note that these tasks are not similar to Ada tasks, but lightweight computation units which will be executed by runtime worker threads.

The work of [9] proposes a similar approach for Ada, where a library of generics is proposed to allow for common parallel patterns in Ada programs.

## 3.2 Pre-processer based approaches

The next example presents the same function using the OpenMP [6] specification, a pre-processor based approach. OpenMP is a specification produced by an industry consortium, based on directives that allow the pre-processor or the compiler to automatically inject the code required to execute the program on top of the parallel runtime.

```
int fib(int n)
{
   if (n < 2) return n;
   int x, y;

   #pragma omp task shared(x)
   x = fib(n - 1);

   #pragma omp task shared(y)
   y = fib(n - 2);

   #pragma omp taskwait
   return x+y;
}
```

**Listing 4 – OpenMP Example**

The example in Listing 4 provides two of these directives. The first, which is used before both recursive calls to the `fib` function notes the pre-processor that the following block of code can be executed in parallel. Thus, `fib(n - 1)` and `fib(n - 2)` can be executed by two parallel threads. The final directive causes the main task to wait for the end of the tasks that it has created. The `shared(x)` information informs the compiler that variable `x` will be accessed by different threads, therefore exclusion algorithms should be used.

The work in [9] also provides a brief proposal how Ada could have a similar approach, by using a set of `pragmas`, with the compiler converting the code to use the generic libraries, thus hiding more complex programming.

## 3.3 Language based approaches

The final example presents the language based approach of Cilk Plus [18], an evolution of Cilk [3] / Cilk++ [19], that provides a very simple and small set of linguistic extensions to C++ to support parallel applications, on top of libraries and runtimes providing work-stealing capabilities. Because it is a small extension, parallelizing existent code is a very easy task.

```
int fib(int n)
{
    if (n < 2) return n;
    int x, y;

    x = cilk_spawn fib(n-1);
    y = fib(n-2);

    cilk_sync;

    return x+y;
}
```

**Listing 5 – Cilk Example**

The `cilk_spawn` keyword in Listing 5 performs the same functionality of the `omp task` directive in the previous sub section, noting the compiler that `fib(n - 1)` can execute in parallel. `cilk_sync` is equivalent to `omp taskwait`.

# 4. A PROPOSAL FOR ADA

In this proposal for Ada, the goal is to maintain the structure of Ada programs, but allowing the programmer to specify code which is potentially parallel, which then the runtime can dynamically during runtime either execute sequentially, or parallelize. The followed approach is a language-based one, as the authors consider it to be more appropriate to the Ada philosophy of supporting concurrency directly at the language level.

In this preliminary work, three constructs are proposed:

- Parallelizable blocks
- Parallelizable functions
- Parallelizable for loops

The proposal introduces two new keywords: `parallel`, which specifies potentially parallel operations, and `future`, which specifies values which are calculated asynchronously.

## 4.1 Parallelizable blocks

Ada's block construct is a natural candidate for declaring potentially parallel code, as it encloses a sequence of statements in a single statement that can be placed anywhere in an Ada program. Furthermore, the variables in the declarative part can be created in the actual core of execution, similar to private variables in OpenMP, allowing for a better utilization of the local caches. Listing 6 provides the structure of the parallel block, which is identified with the `parallel` keyword.

```
-- not legal Ada
declare
   Local_var : ...;
   Local_copy : ... := Global_var;
parallel begin
   -- ...
end parallel;
```

**Listing 6 – Proposal for a parallel block**

Nevertheless, it is important that these "parallel blocks" do not update global variables. This can be allowed, but programmers must understand that the behaviour and performance may be the same as variables being assessed by different tasks in different threads (and different processors), so protected objects should be used. Read only variables may be copied by the programmer in the declarative part, or may be implicitly copied by the compiler.

Since these parallel blocks execute asynchronously with the following code, it is important to determine how the results of the block are used, and it must be possible for the main program to wait for them to be available. A potential solution is to use futures [20], variables which are a placeholder for a future result. Synchronization is only required when the value is actually used. Obviously, for a future to be used, its scope must be enclosing of the parallel block (Listing 7).

```
   -- not legal Ada
   Future_V: future ...;
begin
   -- ...
   declare
      Local_var : ...;
   parallel begin
      -- ...
      -- code that computes Future_V
   end parallel;

   -- asynchronous execution
   Do_Something_Else;
```

```
X := Future_V; -- The result of the
               -- computation is required
               -- Program will wait for
               -- end of parallel block
```

**Listing 7 –parallel block example**

## 4.2 Parallelizable functions

A second construct presented in this paper is a simple way for the programmer to specify that a function can execute in parallel. Therefore, when a call to the function is performed, the underlying runtime can decide to parallelize the call, if there are enough available cores.

For instance, the example in Listing 8 maps the parallel Fibonacci function, as presented in the previous section, with the parallel function construct.

```
-- not legal Ada
parallel function Fibonacci (
                    Value : in Natural)
      return future Natural is
   n1, n2: Natural;
begin
   if Value < 2 then
      return Value;
   n1 := Fibonacci (Value - 1);
   n2 := Fibonacci (Value - 2);
   return n1 + n2;
end parallel Fibonacci;
```

**Listing 8 – Proposal for a parallel function**

Note the use of the `parallel` keyword in the function signature [3], and the specification of the return value as a `future`, as the function may be executed asynchronously, thus the calling code must wait for its completion when the return value is required (Listing 9).

```
 -- not legal Ada
 Fib_Res: future Natural;
begin
 Fib_Res := Fibonacci (10);
 ... -- code in parallel to the
     -- fibonacci function call
 X := Fib_Res; -- The result of the
               -- computation is required
               -- Program will wait for
               -- end of parallel funtion
```

**Listing 7 –parallel block example**

## 4.3 Parallelizable for loops

The last construct that can be paralyzed is the `for loop`. Note that in this case, it is not mandatory that each iteration of the loop is executed in parallel. Efficient runtimes may partition the data set into blocks, and assign each block to a potentially parallel unit (an approach similar to TPL's `Parallel.For` [7]). Listing 10 provides an example of incrementing all elements of an array.

```
-- not legal Ada
for I in Buffer'Range    parallel loop
   Buffer(I) := Buffer(I) + 1;
end parallel loop;
```

**Listing 10 – Proposal for a parallel loop**

A more complex approach is required if the for loop is performing an aggregation (loop iterations are not independent). For example, Listing 11 provides and example of a sequential `for loop`, performing the sum of an array. Obviously, this cannot be parallelized with the same approach as in Listing 9.

```
Sum := 0;
for I in Buffer'Range loop
   Sum := Sum + Buffer(I);
end loop;
```

**Listing 11 – Sequential Sum loop**

The parallelization of this type of loops is only advantageous if there is the capability to do partial sums for array blocks and then performing an aggregate sum in the end. For that, the change to the structure of the `for loop` needs to be more complex.

Note that it is not possible to delegate to the programmer the definition of blocks and partial arrays, as it may be the underlying runtime that determines during the execution the number and size of blocks. But it is necessary for the program to be able to reason in terms of block ranges and partial results. A solution (Listing 12) could be to create specific attributes to arrays, which could be used to know the range of the current block (`Partial_First .. Partial_Last`), and to allow variables to have a `Partial` attribute referring to a local copy in each parallel block. After the end of the `parallel for`, these local copies could be available in an array, accessible by the `Partial_Array` attribute.

```
-- not legal Ada
Sum := 0;
for I in Buffer'Range parallel loop
   for J in Buffer'Partial_First ..
              Buffer'Partial_Last loop
     Sum'Partial := Sum'Partial +
                      Buffer(J);
```

[3] Previously we had considered the `parallel` keyword to be placed after `is`, just before the declaration block, or before `begin`, as in parallel blocks. However, it was later decided to place it in the beginning to be able to more easily define potential parallel functions also at declaration. Aspects were also considered, but using `function X with Parallel` does not convey the correct idea.

```
    end loop;
  end parallel loop;


  for I in Sum'Partial_Array loop
       Sum := Sum + Buffer'Partial(I);
  end loop;
```

**Listing 12 – Proposal for a parallel loop with aggregation**

Note that the code after the `parallel for loop` waits for all parallel iterations to terminate, before being able to execute.

## 4.4 Discussion

The work presented in this paper is still preliminary as there are several issues which need to be considered. For instance, the interaction of parallel computations and the exception model of Ada is complex, as parallel computation may be performed in worker threads, thus in a context which is not of the enclosing task. Also exiting from blocks or loops in recursive parallel computations must take into account the potential need to abort other computations being executed in other threads.

Nevertheless, the three proposed constructs for parallelism mentioned in the previous sections (parallelizable blocks, functions and for-loops), can be the basis for creating a parallel programming model in Ada. In addition, the future keyword can play an important role in synchronization, acting as a join function for different parallel computations that need to meet at some point of execution.

Another area of importance to the design of parallel Ada programs is the data-sharing model. It is interesting to note that asynchronous message passing between parallel code is more and more considered to be an option for highly parallel programs, instead of data-sharing. Another area which needs to be considered is the use of non-blocking data structures or software transactions instead of lock-based data sharing.

Finally, the incorporation in the Ada runtime model of the support to the parallelizable computational units is also of paramount importance. It is thus clear that the definition of the semantics of this model is indeed a challenging (but potentially parallel) task, considering the interaction with all Ada features.

Nevertheless, the provided examples are sufficient to outline how the model could be implemented within the Ada language model (the code still looks Ada), and it is a starting point to foster a discussion on this issue. It is the opinion of the authors that the Ada community must start considering that for the foreseen future platforms (tens or hundreds of cores), the available task model may not scale. The area of programming models for parallel computing is (once again) with immense activity, and Ada should define its model. Both the work presented in this paper, and the generics/pragma implementation of [9] are two directions that can be considered.

# 5. CONCLUSION

The current trend to increase processing power by manufacturing chips including multiple processor cores has popularised the ability to execute concurrent software in parallel. This tendency for even larger number of processor cores will further impact the way systems are developed, as software performance must rely on efficient techniques to design and execute concurrent software in parallel.

This paper discusses some existent approaches to parallel programming using the lightweight thread model, where the programmer specifies a set of potentially parallel computation units, which are then dynamically mapped by the runtime to a set of worker threads, and proposed a draft of how the Ada language could be augmented to support such model.

# 6. ACKNOWLEDGMENTS

We would like to thank the anonymous reviewers for their valuable comments to improve the paper.

This work was supported by the VIPCORE project, ref. FCOMP-01-0124-FEDER-015006, funded by FEDER funds through COMPETE (POFC - Operational Programme 'Thematic Factors of Competitiveness') and by National Funds (PT) through FCT - Portuguese Foundation for Science and Technology, and the ARTISTDESIGN – Network of Excellence on Embedded Systems Design, grant ref. ICT-FP7-214373.

# 7. REFERENCES

[1] H. Sutter and J. Larus, "Software and the concurrency revolution," Queue, vol. 3, pp. 54–62, September 2005.

[2] K. Asanovic, R. Bodik, B. C. Catanzaro, J. J. Gebis, P. Husbands, K. Keutzer, D. A. Patterson, W. L. Plishker, J. Shalf, S. W. Williams, and K. A. Yelick. The landscape of parallel computing research: A view from berkeley. Technical Report UCB/EECS-2006-183, EECS Department, University of California, Berkeley, Dec 2006.

[3] M. Frigo, C. E. Leiserson, and K. H. Randall. The implementation of the cilk-5 multithreaded language. SIGPLAN Not., 33:212-223, May 1998

[4] Intel. Thread Building Blocks, http://threadingbuildingblocks.org/. Last access September 2011.

[5] D. Lea. A java fork/join framework. In Proceedings of the ACM 2000 conference on Java Grande, JAVA '00, pages 36-43, New York, NY, USA, 2000. ACM.

[6] A. Marowka. Parallel computing on any desktop. Commun. ACM, 50:74-78, September 2007.

[7] Microsoft. Task parallel library, http://msdn.microsoft.com/en-us/library/dd460717.aspx. Last access September 2011.

[8] K. Taura, K. Tabata, and A. Yonezawa. Stackthreads/mp: integrating futures into calling standards. ACM SIGPLAN Notices, 34(8):60–71, 1999.

[9] B. Moore, "Parallelism generics for Ada 2005 and beyond", SIGAda'10 Proceedings of the ACM SIGAda annual conference, October 2010.

[10] R. D. Blumofe and C. E. Leiserson. Scheduling multithreaded computations by work stealing. J. ACM, 46:720-748, September 1999.

[11] Moore, B., "A comparison of work-sharing, work-seeking, and work-stealing parallelism strategies using Paraffin with Ada 2005", Ada User Journal, Vol 32, N. 1, March 2011.

[12] A. Burns and A. J. Wellings, "Dispatching Domains for Multiprocessor Platforms and their Representation in Ada," 15th International Conference on Reliable Software Technologies - Ada-Europe 2010, Valencia, Spain, June 14-18, 2010.

[13] H. G. Mayer, S. Jahnichen, "The data-parallel Ada run-time system, simulation and empirical results", Proceedings of Seventh International Parallel Processing Symposium, Aprl 1993, Newport, CA , USA , pp. 621 – 627

[14] M. Hind , E. Schonberg, "Efficient Loop-Level Parallelism in Ada", TriAda 91, October 1991

[15] J. Thornley, "Integrating parallel dataflow programming with the Ada tasking model". In *Proceedings of the conference on TRI-Ada '94* (TRI-Ada '94), Charles B. Engle, Jr. (Ed.). ACM, New York, NY, USA, 417-428, 1994. DOI=10.1145/197694.197742 http://doi.acm.org/10.1145/197694.197742

[16] J. Thornley, "Declarative Ada: parallel dataflow programming in a familiar context". In *Proceedings of the 1995 ACM 23rd annual conference on Computer science* (CSC '95), C. Jinshong Hwang and Betty W. Hwang (Eds.). ACM, New York, NY, USA, 73-80, 1995. DOI=10.1145/259526.259540 http://doi.acm.org/10.1145/259526.259540

[17] R. Harper, "Parallelism is not concurrency", Ropert Harper Blog, http://existentialtype.wordpress.com/ 2011/03/17/parallelism-is-not-concurrency/, Last access September 2011.

[18] Intel, Cilk Plus, http://software.intel.com/en-us/articles/intel-cilk-plus/, Last access September 2011

[19] C. Leiserson, "The Cilk++ concurrency platform", Proceedings of the 46th Annual Design Automation Conference , ACM New York, USA, 2009.

[20] H. Baker, C. Hewitt, "The Incremental Garbage Collection of Processes". Proceedings of the Symposium on Artificial Intelligence Programming Languages, SIGPLAN Notices 12, August 1977.

# Stack Safe Parallel Recursion with Paraffin

Brad J. Moore
General Dynamics Canada
1020 68th Ave. N.E., Calgary, Alberta, Canada
001.403.730.1367
Brad.moore@gdcanada.com

## ABSTRACT

Recursion is a programming technique in which a solution can be expressed by a subroutine invoking itself either directly or indirectly. Many problems can be expressed simply using a recursive approach, however one of the drawbacks of using recursion is that it requires a stack, and often one does not know how much stack space is needed to obtain a recursive result. Stack overflow often results in spectacular failure with strange, often unrepeatable behaviour. Paraffin is a suite of generic units that can add parallelism to iterative and recursive problems. Some of the generics involve a load balancing technique described as "work-seeking". It was found that the recursive work seeking algorithm could be extended to also provide stack safety whereby the generics monitor the amount of remaining stack space and avoid stack overflow using a technique similar to load balancing. The stack safety feature also makes it attractive to consider Paraffin for use with code destined for execution on a single core. This paper describes how the recursive work-seeking algorithm was extended to provide the stack-safety feature, and then goes on to report some performance results using the generics.

## Categories and Subject Descriptors

D.1.3 [**Programming Techniques**]: Concurrent Programming – *parallel programming*; D.3.3 [**Programming Languages**]: Language Constructs and Features – *concurrent programming structures, data types and structures, recursion.*; D.2.13 [**Software Engineering**]: Reusable Software – *reusable libraries*; F.1.2 [**Computation by Abstract Devices**]: Modes of Computation – *parallelism and concurrency*; F.1.2 [**Computation by Abstract Devices**]: Studies of Program Constructs – *program and recursion schemes*; G.1.0 [**Mathematics of Computing**]: Numerical Analysis – *parallel algorithms*.

## General Terms

Algorithms, Performance, Design, Reliability, Standardization, Languages.

## Keywords

Ada 2005, Work-Seeking, Work-Stealing, Work-Sharing, multi-core.



## 1. INTRODUCTION

Multi-core computers are now commonly available and it is expected that the trend for increasing numbers of cores will continue into the future. The processor speeds however have levelled off, so to obtain increased performance, it becomes necessary to consider how to better incorporate parallelism in order to take advantage of these multiple cores. Recently a suite of parallelism generics called "Paraffin" [1] has been made publicly available for Ada 2005 that provides generics for adding parallelism to loops and recursive algorithms. Paraffin has been ported to two different Ada vendors' compilers and generates executables for Windows and Linux operating systems and is intended to be portable to any target that supports Ada 2005 compilation. This paper focuses on Paraffin's recursive generics, and in particular examines the recursive generics that provide so-called stack-safe recursion. The stack-safe algorithm is compared and tested against other recursive generics of Paraffin that do not have the feature.

## 2. PARAFFIN RECURSION GENERICS

For iterative parallelism, Paraffin provides generics that support three difference strategies;

- Work Sharing
- Work Seeking
- Work Stealing

Work Sharing is a basic divide and conquer strategy that divides the work evenly between workers at the start of the parallelism. Work-Seeking and Work-Stealing are load-balancing strategies where idle workers attempt to either "seek" or "steal" work from busy workers. Work-Seeking involves a cooperative hand-off between the idle worker and an offering busy worker, whereas with Work-Stealing, idle workers attempt to steal work from busy workers with minimal task interaction.

For recursive parallelism, Paraffin currently only supports work-sharing and work-seeking generic forms. It is not known if the work-seeking or work-sharing generics could easily be adapted to support work-stealing. Iterative work-stealing is implemented in Paraffin by having the idle worker manipulate the loop exit condition of busy workers. It is not clear how an idle recursive thread could manipulate another recursive thread to steal work in a similar manner without a cooperative approach such as work-seeking.

Of the two recursive strategies, currently only the work-seeking generics provide support for stack-safe recursion. Conceptually, the work-seeking mechanism is a similar capability to stack safety whereby a worker can acquire more work after completion of a work assignment. Future releases of Paraffin may provide the stack-safety feature for work-sharing recursive generics.

The Paraffin generics can be further classified by whether an overall result needs to be produced from the parallelism or not. An overall result is generally not needed if the parallelism only involves iteration through a data structure such as an array or binary tree. An overall result may be needed to provide an output such as a total, minimum, or maximum value for example.

If an overall result is to be generated, then Paraffin reduces the final parallel results from each worker into a single overall result.

Reducing generics exist for both iterative and recursive parallelism in Paraffin. One of the constraints on reduction is that the reducing operation must be associative. An operation is associative if the same result is always obtained for the same set of operands regardless how the operands are grouped together. Addition is an example of an associative operation since;

$(A + B) + C = A + (B + C)$

## 3. PRESERVING OPERATION ORDER

The iterative generic forms preserve the order of operations such that the parallel result should always be identical to the sequential result.

For example, consider a reduction result data type that is a linked list instantiated from Ada.Containers.Doubly_Linked_List whereby the associative reduction operation is one that appends a source list to a target list. One might implement the operation as follows;

```
procedure Reduce
           (Left, Right : in out List) is
begin
   -- Append the Right list to the Left
   Left.Splice
      (Before => Integer_Lists.No_Element,
       Source => Right);
end Reduce;
```

Using this reducer, the iterative result of a loop to append the letters of the alphabet from 'A' to 'Z' to a linked list will result in the expected ordered list when executed in parallel.

```
--  Sequential Code:
--  for Char in 'A' .. 'Z' loop
--     Letter_List.Append
--        (New_Item => Char, Count => 1);
--  end loop
declare
   procedure Iteration
     (Start, Finish : Character;
      Letter_List   : in out
        Doubly_Linked_List_Of_Character.List) is
   begin
      for Char in Start .. Finish loop
         Letter_List.Append (New_Item => Char,
                             Count => 1);
      end loop;
   end Iteration;
begin
   -- Calling Instantiation of Paraffin generic
   Character_Linked_List_Appending_Reducer
     (From         => 'A',
      To           => 'Z',
      Process      => Iteration'Access,
      Item         => Letter_List,
end;
```

Consideration was given for order preservation for the recursive generics, but in order to support this, it would have involved delaying all the reductions until after the completion of the parallelism and using the heap to allocate storage for the intermediate results. If we eliminate the constraint for order preservation for the recursive generics, it greatly simplifies the reduction. Each worker stores its own reduction result for all the work items assigned to the worker, and once all workers have completed their work, computing the final result is simply a matter of reducing the final results of all the workers. As such, workers can perform their own reductions without having to deal with synchronization with other workers. Furthermore the results array can be a bounded array stored on the stack. The number of elements in the result array corresponds to the number of workers.

A consequence of abandoning order preservation for the recursive generics is that it imposes an additional restriction on reducing operations. In addition to the requirement for associativity, the reducing operation also needs to be commutative. An operation is commutative if the operands can be applied in any order to achieve the same result. Addition is an example of a commutative operation, since;

$A + B = B + A.$

For recursive data structures, it typically is not clear what the order should be anyway. For example, a binary tree can be processed with pre-order, in-order, or post-order traversal, and there are other conceivable orders that one could choose for ordering the nodes in a tree.

The previous example involving linked list reduction however is a case where the lack of order preservation could lead to an ordering of nodes that differs from the sequential result. This is not an issue if two lists are considered equal if they both contain the same items (regardless of order), however the usual semantics for a linked list is that equality implies identical node ordering. This in fact is the semantics of the "=" operator for the Ada.Containers.Doubly_Linked_Lists generic.

```
function "="
   (Left, Right : List) return Boolean;
```

If recursive parallelism is desired involving a reduction operation that produces a set of values, a better choice for container would be Ada.Containers.Ordered_Maps since the order is maintained by the container generic, and since two sets are considered equal if they simply contain the same elements.

An associative and commutative reducing operation could then be;

```
procedure Reduce
           (Left, Right : in out Set) is
begin
   Left.Union (Right);
end Reduce;
```

In this case, some analysis may be needed to examine the ordered set implementation to determine if the benefits gained from parallelism are offset by the work involved creating unions from the results of multiple workers.

In summary, it was decided that the performance impact and coding changes needed to implement order preservation was not worthwhile for the recursive generics.

## 4. WORK OFFERS AND DEFERRAL

Prior to implementing the stack-safety feature, the mechanism for assigning work to a work-seeking worker task involved work requests and work offers. An idle worker makes a work request when it is looking for more work, and a busy worker hands off work to a requesting worker by making a work offer to split the busy worker's workload between the busy worker and the idle worker.

Busy workers monitor an atomic Boolean flag that indicates if other workers are seeking work. This flag is checked on each recursive call, and if the flag is set, then a work offer is made by busy workers to the work seeker if the busy worker has work that can be off-loaded to another worker.

The work offer mechanism requires that a worker must be first seeking work before a work offer can be made. The stack-safety feature however requires a slightly different protocol. When a stack alarm threshold is crossed, a busy worker cannot proceed any further with the current work item as it is deemed to be unsafe to risk possible stack overflow. However, there is no guarantee that an idle worker exists at the time the stack alarm is detected for a busy worker, so the possibility for a direct hand-off of work cannot be assumed.

The mechanism for putting a work item aside for later processing is called a work deferral. Work deferrals are implemented as a queue of pending work items. The idea is that a work item that cannot be managed by the current worker results in a copy of the work item being appended to a global work deferral queue shared between all workers. Later, when an idle worker requests more work, a check is first made to see if any deferred work items exist. If work has been deferred, then the idle worker takes the first work item from the work deferral queue rather than request work from a busy worker. This exchange is described in more detail in the following section.

## 5. STACK-SAFETY

The stack safety feature of Paraffin's recursive generics involves monitoring the stack usage and triggering a work deferral if a stack usage threshold is crossed.

The stack-safety feature involves having an idle worker first check the deferred work list to see if there is any deferred work available, before setting the seeking-work flag to request work from other busy workers. If deferred work is available, then the idle worker removes the work item from the head of the deferred work queue and proceeds with that work. Otherwise, the idle worker sets the atomic seeking-work flag, and potentially obtains work in the usual work- seeking manner.

The threshold used to trigger stack-safe work deferral is specified as a percentage of the total stack space, which is a parameter of the generic. A threshold value of 80% means that if the stack usage of a worker exceeds 80%, then the current work item is not processed. If a reduction result is needed, then a special value called the *identity value* is returned by the recursive call allowing the current worker to proceed and unwind its stack as though the real recursive result value had been returned by the call. If a reduction result is not needed, then the recursive call simply returns.

The identity value is a special value known to the generic such that applying the identity value using the reduction operation yields the same result. For example, if the reduction operation is addition, then the identity value is zero. If the reduction operation is multiplication, then the identity value is 1. The identify value for a set union operation would be an empty set.

When an idle worker picks up a work item from the deferred work queue, it starts processing the work item with a fresh, empty stack, allowing the work to proceed as before until either the work item has either been completely processed, or the stack limit threshold is again reached and processed in a similar fashion.

When a worker completes its work assignment, it reduces its result, if any, into an overall result array at an index corresponding to the worker. The final result for the overall work given to a worker is reduced into the overall result for all workers once all workers have completed all their work assignments.

The stack size of the workers can also be specified by a parameter to the generic. Internally, this translates to the value used on a Storage_Size pragma within the generic, for the definition of the worker tasks.

Note that the stack-safety feature does not absolutely guarantee that stack overflows will not occur. If the amount of stack space utilized in a single recursive call is greater than the amount of stack space between the stack alarm threshold address and the top of the stack, then an overflow could occur before the overflow check can be made. This ordinarily isn't a possibility since each recursive call typically only uses a very small fragment of the remaining stack space. It usually is the occurrence of a large number of recursive calls that lead to stack overflow situations. If this is a concern for a particular recursive problem, static analysis tools may help to determine the safety of the overall operation, and to confirm that the amount of stack usage for a single recursive call is well below the difference between the top of the stack and the stack alarm threshold address.

## 6. WORK-DEFERRAL OVERHEAD

The test results reported in this paper show results for cases that do not involve work-deferral. The intent is to compare the stack-safe algorithm against other generic forms that do not have the feature.

When work-deferrals do occur, they incur additional overhead.

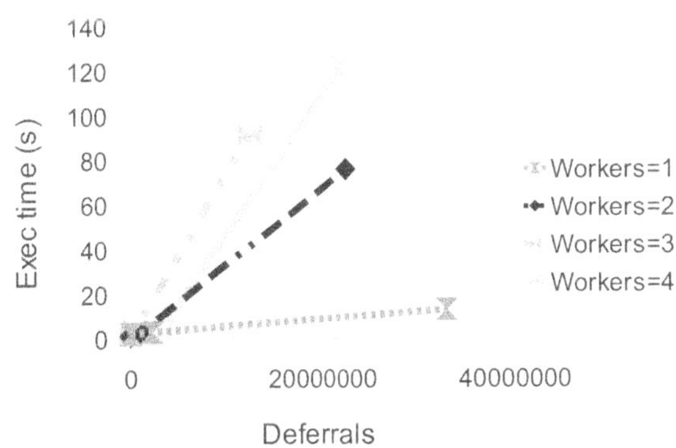


**Figure 1: Work Deferral Performance Impact**

Testing has shown that if the number of work-deferrals is relatively small, the performance differences are negligible. However, if the number of work-deferrals is high, (e.g. 100000's of deferrals) the performance can degrade significantly.

With recursion, the number of deferrals can be very sensitive to stack size and alarm threshold settings. Figure 1 shows the number of deferrals that occurred calculating the Fibonacci value for 40 using a stack size of 16#4000# and a stack threshold value ranging from 12% - 16%, with 16% resulting in no stack deferrals, and 12% generating deferrals in the range of 20,000,000 to 40,000,000.

For four workers with four cores, the performance was relatively unaffected when the number of deferrals ranged between 0 and 1000 (0.59 seconds – 0.68 seconds). Between 1000 and 10000 deferrals the performance degraded to 1.47 seconds, and from 10000 and 4,000,000 the performance dropped to 10 seconds.

Paraffin's strategy can be described as a 'better safe than sorry' approach. To this end, Paraffin's stack-safe generics include an out parameter that provides a count of the number of stack-alarm threshold crossings (work deferrals) that occurred during the parallel processing. This value can be checked dynamically, such that the stack size (an in parameter to the generic procedure) can be increased to eliminate the alarms for subsequent calls to the recursive generic.

## 7. FIBONACCI EXAMPLE

Recall that the Fibonacci sequence can be defined recursively such that the Fibonacci value of n is equal to the Fibonacci value of (n – 1) plus the Fibonacci value of (n – 2).

A sequential implementation for this in Ada could be;

```
function Fibonacci
  (Value : Natural) return Natural is
begin
   if Value < 2 then
      return Value;
   else
      return Fibonacci (Value - 2) +
             Fibonacci (Value - 1);
   end if;
end Fibonacci;
```

Applying Paraffin's work-seeking generics involves a simple transformation of the sequential code that includes enclosing the sequential code with a few lines of wrapper code that invokes the Paraffin generic.

After applying Paraffin's work-seeking generic to add parallelism to this code, the resulting implementation becomes;

```
with Parallel.Recursion.
    Elementary_Work_Seeking_Reducing_Recurse;
use Parallel;

function Fibonacci
   (Value : Natural) return Natural is

 Other_Workers : aliased Work_Seeking_State;

 type Recursion_Routine is access function
    (Number : Natural) return Natural;

 Recurse : aliased Recursion_Routine := null;

 function Parallel_Fibonacci
   (Number : Natural) return Natural is
 begin

   if Number < 2 then return Number;
   elsif Other_Workers.Seeking_Work then
                - In parallel
      return
         Recurse (Number - 2) +
         Parallel_Fibonacci (Number - 1);
   else         - Sequentially
      return
         Parallel_Fibonacci (Number - 2) +
         Parallel_Fibonacci (Number - 1);
   end if;
 end Parallel_Fibonacci;

 function Recursive_Integer_Addition
   is new Parallel.Recursion.
     Elementary_Work_Seeking_Reducing_Recurse
    (Work_Type => Natural,
     Result_Type => Natural,
     Reducer => "+",
     Identity_Value => 0,
     Recursion_Routine => Recursion_Routine);

begin
   return Recursive_Integer_Addition
     (Item  => Value,
      Other_Workers => Other_Workers'Access,
      Recursion => Recurse'Access,
      Process => Parallel_Fibonacci'Access);
end Fibonacci_Elementary_Work_Seeking;
```

The *Recurse* variable is an access-to-subprogram that is initialized by the Paraffin generic. It is to be called by the client code when recursing once a parallelism opportunity has been detected, by checking the Other_Workers.Seeking_Work Boolean flag.

The work item passed as a parameter to *Recurse* is called a work offer, and if accepted by the generic, means that the work item has been handed to another worker and a special value called the identity value described above is returned to the worker that made the offer.

Thus, the worker that made the work offer continues as though it received a sequential result by calling itself recursively. On the other hand, if the work item is not accepted, such as might be the case if another worker made an earlier offer to the idle worker, then the *Recurse* routine ends up calling the sequential subroutine recursively.

The *Recurse* subprogram should only be called for one branch of the recursion. This is because typically there is only one idle worker seeking work, and so generally it makes sense to only make a single work offer. This also allows the current worker to continue with other branches of the recursion without incurring the overhead of an extra work offer that likely wouldn't have been accepted anyway. The call to *Recurse* should be made before the other branches of recursion, since in order for the work to proceed in parallel, the call that passes off work to another worker should happen before starting the sequential recursive branches.

Note also that the instantiation of the generic, *Recursive_Integer_Addition* does not necessarily need to be enclosed and included with the client code. For example, if parallel recursive reduction of integers occurs in other places in an application then the instantiation and the *Recursion_Routine* type definition could be placed in a library level package and shared between the various locations in the code by being mentioned in a **with** clause.

## 8. STACK SAFE EXAMPLE

As mentioned previously, stack safety involves checking the amount of remaining stack space during each recursive call and then deferring the work item for later processing if stack resources are dangerously low. Extending the recursive work-seeking generics to have this capability involved having the generic pass a stack limit threshold value to the client code. The stack limit threshold is simply a machine address of a stack location that is determined via an offset into the worker's stack, based on a percentage of the stack size and the address of the base of the stack.

To provide stack-safety, the client code should check the address of a local variable (typically a work item parameter) against the stack limit address. If the address is less than the stack limit, then it implies the stack threshold limit has been crossed. The previous example is now extended to include the work deferral logic, so that *Recurse* is called by the client when either making a work offer to an idle worker, or deferring work due to reaching the stack limit threshold. Using the Stack-Safe generic, the Fibonacci example now becomes;

```
with Parallel.Recursion.
Stack_Safe_Elementary_Work_Seeking_Reducing_Recurse
;
use Parallel;

function Fibonacci
   (Value : Natural) return Natural is

 Other_Workers : aliased Work_Seeking_State;

 type Recursion_Routine is access function
     (Number : Natural;
      Stack_Limit : System.Address)
        return Natural;

 Recurse : aliased Recursion_Routine := null;

 function Parallel_Fibonacci
    (Number : Natural;
     Stack_Limit : System.Address)
           return Natural is
 begin

   if Number < 2 then return Number;
   elsif Other_Workers.Seeking_Work then
                 - In parallel
      return
         Recurse (Number - 2) +
         Parallel_Fibonacci (Number - 1);
   elsif Number'Address <= Stack_Limit then
                 - Defer work
      return
         Recurse (Number - 2) +
         Recurse (Number - 1);
   else          - Sequentially
      return
         Parallel_Fibonacci (Number - 2) +
         Parallel_Fibonacci (Number - 1);
   end if;
 end Parallel_Fibonacci;

 function Stack_Safe_Integer_Addition
   is new Parallel.Recursion.Stack_Safe_
     Elementary_Work_Seeking_Reducing_Recurse
    (Work_Type => Natural,
     Result_Type => Natural,
     Reducer => "+",
     Identity_Value => 0,
     Recursion_Routine => Recursion_Routine);

begin
   return Stack_Safe_Integer_Addition
     (Item   => Value,
      Other_Workers => Other_Workers'Access,
      Recursion => Recurse'Access,
      Process => Parallel_Fibonacci'Access,
      Max_Depth => 80,   - percentage
      Storage_Size => 16#8000#);
end Fibonacci_Elementary_Work_Seeking;
```

The other differences are that the generic allows the stack limit threshold to be specified as a percentage, and the stack size of the workers can be specified via the Storage_Size parameter, which translates to a Storage_Size pragma (or aspect for Ada 2012) being applied to the worker task definition within the generic.

Note also that if the stack threshold has been crossed, then the *Recurse* subprogram is called for all recursive branches, not just one as is the case for work offers. This is needed because if the stack threshold is crossed for one branch of recursion, it likely will also be crossed for other recursive branches. The *Recurse* routine needs to be called for all recursive branches to ensure that the corresponding work items are deferred for later processing.

## 9. WORK-SEEKING SPEED BOOST

Previously [2][3], it had been reported that work-seeking generally outperformed or performed comparably with work-sharing generics in all recursive tests except the Fibonacci tests. At the time, no explanation was given why work-seeking performance gave poor results for that test only. Digging deeper it was discovered that the reason this test fared so poorly was because too many work offers were being made for work at the bottom of the recursion. Presumably, Fibonacci recursion is more of a balanced problem than iterating through a Red-Black tree [6] such that both branches of recursion typically end up completing at roughly the same time.

When an idle worker requested more work, it would be more likely to receive work offers from other tasks that had almost completed their respective work assignments. Essentially, too many poor work offerings were being made, leading to a high degree of work handoffs which incurred higher overhead than sequential processing. The Red-Black tree problem however is more of an unbalanced problem, which meant that when an idle worker requested more work, chances were more likely that sizeable work items were being offered to the idle task. Intuitively, this explains why the binary tree based tests resulted in good test results.

It was found that performance can be significantly improved if a mechanism can be provided to allow the client code to avoid making work offers that are too deep in the recursive call hierarchy.

Paraffin allows for two different approaches. Both are filtering approaches. One approach filters out potential work offers based on the amount of work remaining for a given worker, whereas the other approach involves filtering out potential offers based on the amount of work already performed by the worker. (A stack-depth based test)

Computing Fibonacci values is a problem for which either approach may be applied. One can judge the amount of work remaining by examining the current Fibonacci value. As the value approaches 0, the desirability of making a work offer lessens.

This check can be added to the client code without requiring any modifications to the Paraffin generics. For example, it was found that Fibonacci work offers were not worth making for computing Fibonacci numbers less than about 20. This filtering can be accomplished by adding a simple check to the Fibonacci client code that checks for work offers.

```
if Number < 2 then return Number;
elsif Other_Workers.Seeking_Work
  and then Number >= 20 then
     return
        Recurse (Number - 2) +
        Parallel_Fibonacci (Number - 1);
```

This approach works for recursive problems that involve convergence towards the recursion exit criteria, where the decision to make a work offer can be calculated based on how close the execution is to reaching the convergence point. For many recursive problems however, it is not possible to gauge how much recursion remains for a given worker. For this sort of problem, a reasonable alternative to knowing how much work remains, is to know how much work has been done.

A rough approximation can be obtained if one examines the depth of the recursion. The depth of the recursion can generally be provided, and so Paraffin generic versions exist that provide the stack depth. This is an extra parameter provided on each recursive call and thus does introduce some additional overhead, although testing has shown that the performance differences are not very significant. The performance gain associated with eliminating poor work offers however has been shown to make a very notable difference. For the Fibonacci problem, it was found that cutting off the depth at a value of around 10 provided good performance benefits. The client code can be modified to provide the filtering as shown below. For the stack-depth filtering approach it was found that a value of 10 seemed to also work equally well for solving different values of Fibonacci. This suggests that it may be a good general limit to use and may possibly work well for other recursive problems, though further testing would be needed to determine if such a generalization can be made.

```
if Number < 2 then return Number;
elsif Other_Workers.Seeking_Work
  and then Stack_Depth <= 10 then
     return Recurse (Number - 2) +
       Parallel_Fibonacci (Number - 1);
```

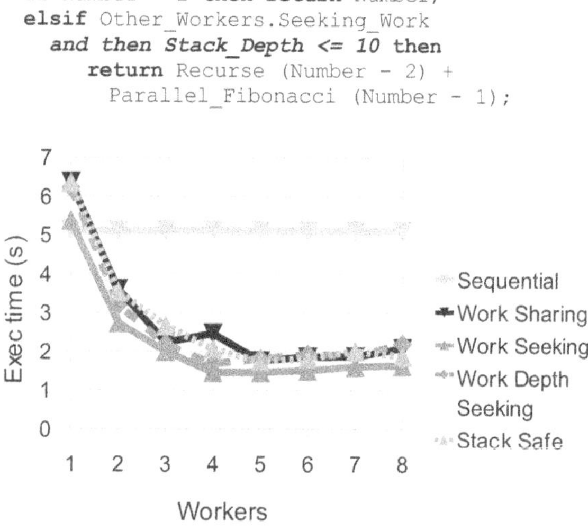


**Figure 2: Work Offer Filtering Comparison**

These results shows the differences between work-seeking using the work-remaining filtering, work-seeking using the work-completed depth filtering, as well as work-sharing and stack safe work-seeking using the work-remaining filtering. While plain work-seeking with work-remaining filtering provided the best results, the other variants are shown to provide similar results on a Linux work station with four cores. This suggests that the stack safety feature may be worth general consideration, as the performance is not greatly affected yet the safety of the processing is greatly improved.

# 10. TEST RESULTS

The following test results were collected using a desktop computer running Ubuntu 11.04 Linux Kernel 2.6.38-10 on an AMD Athlon II X4 635 Processor. The code was compiled using the Adacore GNAT GPL 2011 version of the compiler. No optimization was used in the compiler switches for the project, although the Suppress_All_Checks flag was enabled.

Similar results can be obtained with the Suppress_All_Checks flag disabled, though the overall performance is slower, since the additional safety associated with range checking does typically introduce overhead that seems to be evenly applied to all versions of the code including the sequential version. These tests only exercise the recursive generics of Paraffin. The recursive generics currently only support work-sharing, work-seeking, and stack-safe work-seeking forms of parallelism, so the test results will only compare these strategies.

## Recursive Iteration through a Red-Black Tree

This problem involves iterating through the nodes of a binary red-black tree containing 100_000 nodes.

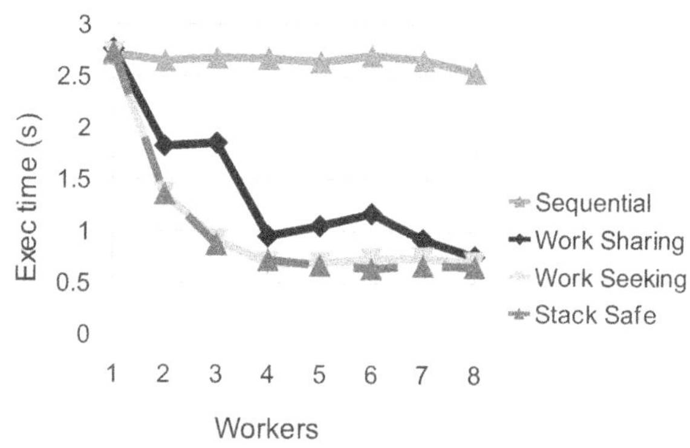


**Figure 3: Parallel Recursion through tree**

A red-black tree can be considered to be a reasonably balanced tree, but there will always be more nodes on one side of the tree than the other, so it makes sense that a work-seeking approach would perform better because the processing loads are actually unbalanced. It is interesting to note that the stack-safe generic ran marginally faster than the plain work-seeking generic, which is surprising because there should be some extra overhead associated with checking the stack usage.

## Recursive Reduction of tree nodes

This test involves calculating the sum of all 100000 nodes in a red-black binary tree container. Each node contains an integer value that is examined by the recursive generics to produce the final result.

The results shown in Figure 4 are similar to the previous recursive iteration example. Work-Seeking clearly performs better than work-sharing for this test and there does not appear to be any noticeable performance impact on using the stack safe version of the generic.

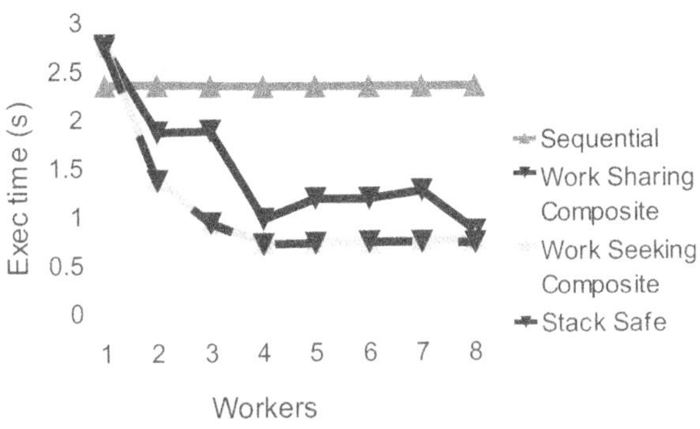


**Figure 4: Parallel Reduction through tree**

### 3.3 Recursive Fibonacci

This test involves applying the paraffin recursive generics to generate Fibonacci numbers in parallel.

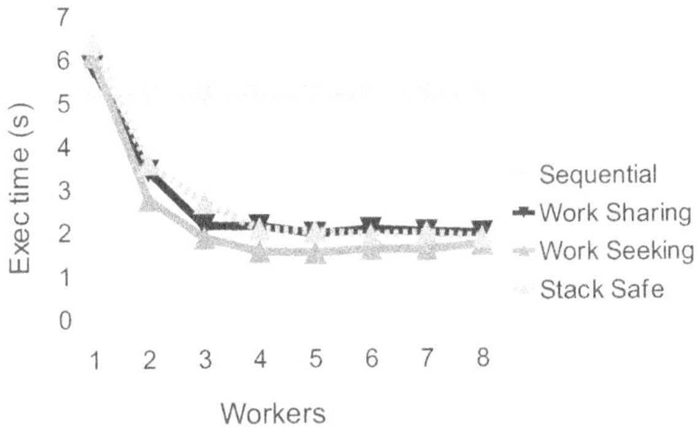


**Figure 5: Parallel Recursive Fibonacci**

Here we now see that work seeking outperforms work-sharing, even though the problem is considered to involve more of a balanced workload. All forms of the generic, including the stack-safe version performed comparably well.

### 3.4 Recursive Integration

This test involves integrating a mathematical function using a recursive trapezoidal integration algorithm [4].

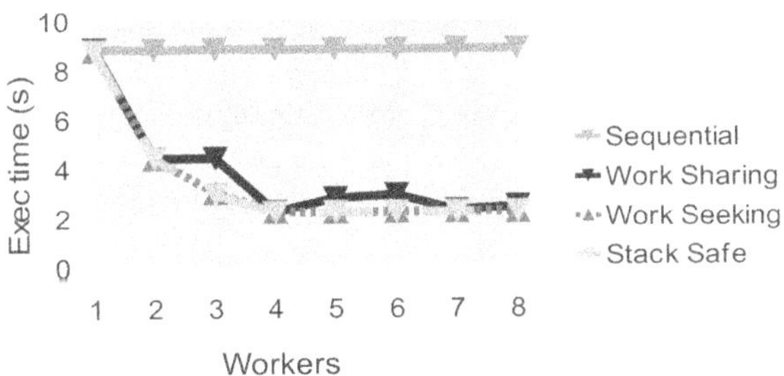


**Figure 6: Parallel Recursive Integration**

In this case, the test involves integrating the square root function from 1.0000 to 1.00001.

Once again we see in figure 6 that work-seeking provides the best results, and in this case, the stack-safe work-seeking provided results that were mostly indistinguishable from the regular work-seeking form.

## 11. CONCLUSIONS

The testing performed on Paraffin's iterative parallelism generics have previously shown that the work-seeking generic forms are a good, consistent choice when compared to work-sharing and work-stealing forms. Now that Paraffin's recursive generics have incorporated logic to avoid making poor work offers, testing has now shown that the work-seeking recursive forms also perform consistently better than the work sharing forms, thus the work-seeking recursive generics can be generally recommended for use for both iterative and recursive parallelism. The stack-safe versions of the work-seeking recursive forms have been shown to consistently provide results that closely approximate the results generated for versions that do not have the stack-safety feature. In several cases the results are indistinguishable. The stack-safety feature could also then be recommended generally for use, as any performance trade-offs may be worthwhile in exchange for the robustness and safety offered by the stack-safety feature. Comparing the performance of sequential code without Paraffin generics on a mono-processor, we see that the sequential code sometimes has an edge in performance, though the performance of the Paraffin generic version is comparable enough to consider for use; in particular, the gains in stack-safety may alone make for a good trade-off for slight performance degradation, even for single core processors.

Paraffin source code can be obtained from SourceForge at http://sourceforge.net/projects/paraffin/, under the modified GNAT GPL license.

## 12. ACKNOWLEDGEMENTS

Thanks to General Dynamics for providing support to attend SIGAda 2011 to present this paper.

## 13. REFERENCES

[1] Moore B., Paraffin, http://sourceforge.net/projects/paraffin/ (Sept 2011)

[2] Moore B., Parallelism Generics for Ada 2005 and Beyond, ACM SIGAda '10 (2010)

[3] Moore B., A comparison of work-sharing, work-seeking, and work-stealing parallelism strategies using Paraffin with Ada 2005. Ada User Journal Volume 32, Number 1, March 2011

[4] Fox, G., Williams, R., Messina G., Parallel Computing Works!, ISBN 1-55860-253-4 Morgan Kaufmann Publishers, Inc. 1994

[5] Taft, S.T., Duff, R. A., Brukardt, R.L. And Plödereder, E. Eds (2000). Consolidated Ada Reference Manual. LNCS 2219, Springer-Verlag

[6] Walker J., Red Black Trees, http://www.eternallyconfuzzled.com/tuts/datastructures/jsw_tut_rbtree.aspx (Aug 2010)

[7] Frigo M., Halpern P., Leiserson C., and Lewin- Berlin S., Reducers and Other Cilk++ Hyperobjects. ACM SPAA '09 (2009)

[8] Burns, A., Wellings A., Concurrent and Real-Time Programming in Ada, Cambridge University Press, 2007

[9] Barney Blaise, Lawrence Livermore National Laboratory, https://computing.llnl.gov/tutorials/openMP/#WorkSharing (Sept 2010)

## SIGAda'11 Panel Summary

# How to Make Ada Go Viral

Jean-Pierre Rosen
Adalog
Issy-Les-Moulineaux, France
rosen@adalog.fr

Brad Moore
General Dynamics Canada
Calgary, Alberta, Canada
brad.moore@gdcanada.com

Tucker Taft
Sofcheck
Burlington, MA, USA
stt@sofcheck.com

## Abstract

Every Ada user wonders why Ada does not enjoy the popularity it deserves. Experience shows that once people have been properly trained to it, they generally don't want to return to other languages – but getting the word to the public-at-large – marketing - has always been a weak point of Ada.

Can we change this situation? Recent indicators, like the ?? language popularity rating, shows some positive indication, with Ada's popularity fast rising. This panel brings together experts with various backgrounds to share their views on how to make Ada more mainstream.

*Brad Moore's position*

It is easy to make the claim that Ada is an underrated programming language. It's advocates believe that the language has much to offer in comparison with other mainstream languages, yet the lions share of the market is held by the C based languages (C, C++, Java, C#)[1]. What can be done to bring Ada closer to the forefront? Currently, there are two notable trends in computer architecture. Multicore and miniaturization (data tables, cell phones, etc). What does Ada have to offer in these two arenas? How might Ada adapt to these new architectures? What exciting new features will Ada 2012 bring to the table in this regard? What avenues can be pursued to open new channels for Ada acceptance? Can Ada's resilience to vulnerabilities become a factor, as society demands more safeguards against identity thefts, viruses, and computer crime? Will society demand higher standards for safety and security in financial, medical, automotive, and industry? Does Ada need to go viral, or should the goal instead be to facilitate a slow but steady shift towards Ada? These are some of the questions that need to be explored if we want Ada to sharpen the current trend towards increasing popularity.

*Tucker Taft's position*

The ideas behind the Ada language, which help make Ada programs safer, more secure, and more robust, are more important than ever. Software is representing progressively more and more of the value of systems, including systems that are safety-critical or high security. However, the Ada language itself may no longer be the best vehicle for carrying its ideas into the wider marketplace. The language was originally designed when most computers were mono-processors running at less than 1 MHz, and the defense industry was the biggest developer of complex high-integrity systems. We are entering an era when most computers have multiple cores each running in the 3GHz range, and we are surrounded by commercial systems where complex high-integrity software is fundamental to their safe, secure, and correct functioning.

**Categories & Subject Descriptors:** K.1 [THE COMPUTER INDUSTRY]: Markets.

**General Terms:** Languages.

**Keywords:** Ada, Advocacy

## Bios:

### Jean-Pierre Rosen

JP Rosen is a professional teacher, teaching Ada (since 1979, it was preliminary Ada!), methods, and software engineering. He runs Adalog, a company specialized in providing training, consultancy, and services in all areas connected to the Ada language and software engineering. He is chairman of AFNOR's (French standardization body) Ada group, AFNOR's spokeperson at WG9, member of the Vulnerabilities group of WG9, and chairman of Ada-France.

***Other speaker TBA***


*SIGAda'11*, November 6–10, 2011, Denver, Colorado, USA.
ACM 978-1-4503-1028-4/11/11.

## Keynote Address

# Why I Came Back to Ada

Martin C. Carlisle
Department of Computer Science
2354 Fairchild Dr, Suite 6K41
USAF Academy, CO 80840
martin.carlisle@usafa.edu

### Abstract

After the Air Force Academy switched its curriculum to Java, I extracted myself from the Ada community and moved on to other research interests, particularly computer security. In this talk, I'll explain the new developments that brought me back to Ada and how Ada and SPARK may be a secret weapon in the 21st century.

**Categories & Subject Descriptors:** D. Software, D.3 Programming Languages, D.3.3 Language Constructs and Features, Nouns: Ada. F. Theory of Computation, F.3 Logics and Meanings of Programs, F.3.1 Specifying and Verifying and Reasoning about Programs.

**General Terms:** Languages, Security.

**Keywords:** SPARK, Formal Methods.

### Bio

Martin C. Carlisle is a Professor of Computer Science at the USAF Academy in Colorado Springs, CO, USA. He has a Bachelor of Science in mathematics and computer science from the University of Delaware, and a Master of Arts and Doctor of Philosophy in computer science from Princeton University. He has made numerous contributions to the Ada community, and is most well-known for AdaGIDE, an integrated development environment for GNAT on Windows, and A#, which compiles Ada to .NET. He has received both the SIGAda Outstanding Community Contribution and Distinguished Service awards. He has been named an ACM Distinguished Educator, the CASE Colorado Professor of the Year and the US Air Force Academy Outstanding Science and Engineering Educator and was awarded the US Air Force Exemplary Civilian Service Award.


*SIGAda'11*, November 6–10, 2011, Denver, Colorado, USA.
ACM 978-1-4503-1028-4/11/11.

# Software Vulnerabilities Precluded by SPARK

Joyce L. Tokar, PhD
Pyrrhus Software
PO Box 1352
Phoenix, AZ 85001-1352
+1-480-951-1019
tokar@pyrrhusoft.com

F. David Jones
Pyrrhus Software
PO Box 1352
Phoenix, AZ 85001-1352
+1-480-951-1019
jones@pyrrhusoft.com

Paul E. Black, PhD
National Institute of Standards
100 Bureau Drive, Stop 8970
Gaithersburg, MD 20899-8970
+1 301-975-4794
paul.black@nist.gov

Chris E. Dupilka
National Security Agency
9800 Savage Road, Suite 6511
Fort Meade, MD 20755
+1-301-688-0993
cedupil@orion.ncsc.mil

## ABSTRACT

Software vulnerabilities are defined as a property of a system's security requirements, design, implementation, or operation that could be accidentally triggered or intentionally exploited and result in a security failure [1]. Many organizations throughout the world are studying software vulnerabilities and how they allow software applications to be infiltrated and corrupted. The Common Weakness Enumeration (CWE) [2] is a collection of standard, measurable weaknesses that may be used to assess software tools and services. The CWE may be also be used to document known vulnerabilities and improve communication between parties working on software assurance.

The SPARK programming language and toolset [3, 4] is designed for the development of high assurance software. The SPARK programming language is a subset of the Ada programming language plus a collection of annotations intended to provide a programming language that is unambiguous, free from implementation dependencies, and formally defined. Used together, the SPARK language and toolset enable the prevention and elimination of defects in source code during the development of the code.

This paper presents an analysis of the SPARK programming language against a collection of CWEs.

## Categories and Subject Descriptors

C.2 [**Computer-Communication Networks**]: General [Security and protection]; D.2 [**Software Engineering**]: Software/Program Verification: *Assertion Checkers, Class invariants, Correctness Proofs, Formal Methods, Programming by Contract*; K.6.5 [**Management of Computing and Information Systems**]: Security and Protection

## General Terms

Design, Documentation, Languages, Performance, Reliability, Security, Verification.

## Keywords

CWE, Common Weaknesses, Correctness by Construction, SPARK, SPARK Ada, Software Vulnerabilities.


*SIGAda'11*, November 6–10, 2011, Denver, Colorado, USA.
Copyright 2011 ACM 978-1-4503-1028-4/11/11...$10.00.

## 1. INTRODUCTION

Software vulnerabilities are defined as a property of a system's security requirements, design, implementation, or operation that could be accidentally triggered or intentionally exploited and result in a security failure [1]. Many organizations throughout the world are studying software vulnerabilities and how they allow software applications to be infiltrated and corrupted. The Common Weakness Enumeration (CWE) [2] is a collection of standard, measurable weaknesses that may be used to assess software tools and services. The CWE may be also be used to document known vulnerabilities and improve communication between parties working on software assurance.

For example, buffer overflow is a weakness where a program uses a variable, but erroneously writes to memory outside the space allocated to that variable (CWE 122). This may occur in programs written in the C language, for instance, if ten words are allocated, but the program writes to an "eleventh" word. Programmers should take care that this never happens, but programmers are human and make mistakes. Software tools exist that either try to check that this never happens before the code is executed or instrument the code to detect such an overflow when the program runs. Such programs take extra resources to use and extra diligence to make sure any reported weaknesses are eliminated. In contrast more recently developed programming languages preclude buffer overflows altogether. That is, the programmer cannot express such an erroneous concept or the compilation and execution infrastructure prevents it.

The SPARK programming language and toolset [3, 4] is designed for the development of high assurance software. The SPARK programming language is a subset of the Ada programming language plus a collection of annotations intended to provide a programming language that is unambiguous, free from implementation dependencies, and formally defined. Used together, the SPARK language and toolset enable the prevention and elimination of defects in source code during the development of the code.

This article evaluates the SPARK programming language and toolset against the following CWEs[1]:

- 78 OS Command Injection
- 80 Basic XSS
- 89 SQL Injection
- 99 Resource Injection
- 121 Stack-based Buffer Overflow

[1] This paper is an update to the material that was presented at the HCSS conference in May 2011.

122 Heap-based Buffer Overflow

134 Uncontrolled Format String

170 Improper Null Termination

244 Failure to Clear Heap Memory Before Release ('Heap Inspection')

251 Often Misused: String Management

259 Hard-Coded Password

367 Time-of-check Time-of-use (TOCTOU) Race Condition

391 Unchecked Error Condition

401 Failure to Release Memory Before Removing Last Reference ('Memory Leak')

412 Unrestricted Externally Accessible Lock

415 Double Free

416 Use After Free

457 Use of Uninitialized Variable

468 Incorrect Pointer Scaling

476 NULL Pointer Dereference

489 Leftover Debug Code

## 2. THE SPARK PROGRAMMING LANGUAGE AND TOOLSET

Ada [6] is a widely-used language which is strongly typed. The SPARK language was originally concerned with providing an unambiguous subset of Ada that was suitable for rigorous static analysis and formal verification. The SPARK language is a strict subset of Ada that has unambiguous semantics. The subset is augmented with SPARK annotations that specify contracts on the properties of the code being developed. A program may be examined statically, that is before run time, and properties checked and analyzed to prove the correctness of the code being developed.

The SPARK toolset comprises the Examiner, the Simplifier, and the Proof Checker. The Examiner is an automated static-semantic checker of code characteristics such as type alignment and visibility. It also offers control, data, and information flow analyses which enable the detection of erroneous constructs in a program such as dead code, undefined variables, redundant tests, and ineffective statements. The Simplifier is an automated theorem prover that supplies proof of particular program properties such as the absences of run-time errors, proof of invariant properties, and formal code verification of partial correctness with respect to the formal specification. The SPARK Proof Checker is an interactive proof tool that offers the same capabilities as the Simplifier.

For concurrent programs, the RavenSPARK option adds the Ada Ravenscar tasking profile [5] to the SPARK language. RavenSPARK provides for the design and development of concurrent software with the same level of verification and assurance that is available with SPARK. In addition, RavenSPARK applications are amenable to the static analysis of worst-case execution time (WCET), schedulability, and memory consumption of multi-threaded applications. (Note, static analysis of WCET and memory consumption were explicit design goals of the SPARK language from the start.)

The development cycle of SPARK program utilizing the SPARK tool set generally proceeds as follows:

1. Write SPARK source code.
2. Analyze SPARK source code with the SPARK Examiner. The Examiner checks the syntax and semantics of the source code. The Examiner also generates verification conditions (VCs). The Examiner operates without any user interaction.
3. The SPARK Simplifier does automatic discharging of the VCs. All the really powerful reasoning in the Simplifier. The Simplifier operates without any user interaction.
4. At this stage there are three options available to the developer:
    a. Manually review the remaining VCs and create "proof review" (PRV) files;
    b. Create user-defined proof rules and re-run Simplifier until 100% of the VCs are automatically discharged;
    c. Interactively discharge any remaining VCs using the SPARK Proof Checker.
5. Compile, link, and bind SPARK source code using any Ada compiler. This produces an executable.

It is important to remember that SPARK or RavenSPARK are subsets of Ada; they are not compilation systems. The Examiner verifies that code packages adhere to the subsets but in addition proves that they are correct. A correctness proof requires the special annotations for the Examiner to reason about the source code. Finally the code is run through a normal Ada compiler to produce executable programs.

## 3. COMMON WEAKNESSES AND SPARK

The analysis of the SPARK language for the occurrence of the CWEs identified in Section 1 resulted in a classification of the CWEs with respect to SPARK:

- Class 1: Weaknesses that Cannot Occur
- Class 2: Weaknesses that Can Be Certainly Excluded
- Class 3: Weaknesses that May Occur
- Class 4: Concurrent Programming Weaknesses

Since Class 1 weaknesses cannot even be expressed in syntactically correct SPARK code, no check is needed for them, assuming the compiler conforms to the standard.

Class 2 weaknesses are those that may exist in a SPARK program, and are detectable by the SPARK toolset. These weaknesses may be mitigated by the use of the SPARK toolset to resolve the verification conditions (VCs) associated with the SPARK code. If VCs are not discharged, then such weaknesses may be present in the SPARK code. Otherwise the weaknesses cannot exist in a SPARK program.

Class 3 is collection of weaknesses that may occur in a SPARK program. These are at a semantically higher level. As an example, CWE 489, Left Over Debug Code, can exist in any language. Without the application-specific requirements, it is not possible to determine whether an option to display tables is code for debugging left from development or is a desired behavior of the program. Although a well-defined language may make it easier to determine with certainty that some behavior is or is not present in the program, SPARK does nothing, indeed cannot do anything, directly to preclude class 3 weaknesses from occurring.

Class 4 is a set of weaknesses associated with concurrent programming.

Section 4 discusses Class 1 weaknesses, those that cannot occur in SPARK. Section 5 discusses Class 2 weaknesses, those that might occur, but can be certainly detected by the compiler and examiner. Class 3 weaknesses, those that may occur, are listed in section 6. Section 7 describes the weaknesses associated with concurrency and how SPARK addresses these weaknesses. Where appropriate we discuss nuances of the weakness in SPARK. Section 8 has a summary of all weaknesses.

# 4. Classs 1: Weaknesses that Cannot Occur

This section identifies the weaknesses that cannot occur in SPARK and explains why.

## 4.1 Pointer and Heap Storage Weaknesses Cannot Occur (CWEs 122, 244, 401, 415, 416, 468, and 476)

In SPARK, pointer types and heap storage are disallowed. Immediately, CWEs 122, 244, 401, 415, 416, 468, and 476 are eliminated. Further commentary on CWEs 244 and 476 is appropriate.

### *4.1.1 Heap overflow (CWE 122)*

A heap overflow is a buffer overflow where the buffer is allocated in the heap portion of memory, generally meaning that the buffer was allocated using a routine such as `malloc()`.

This weakness cannot exist in a SPARK program as heap memory does not exist in a SPARK program.

### *4.1.2 Memory leak (CWE 401)*

Memory is allocated, but is not released after it has been used which slowly consumes remaining memory.

This weakness cannot exist in a SPARK program as memory is not allocated dynamically.

### *4.1.3 Double Free (CWE 415)*

When a program calls `free()` twice with the same argument, the program's memory management data structures may become corrupted. This corruption can cause the program to crash or cause later allocations to return the same memory.

This weakness cannot exist in a SPARK program as memory is not allocated dynamically.

### *4.1.4 Use After Free (CWE 416)*

An attempt is made to access the same memory address previously released by a call to `free()`. Referencing memory after it has been freed, and possibly allocated, can cause a program to crash or use unexpected values.

This weakness cannot exist in a SPARK program as memory is not allocated dynamically.

### *4.1.5 Unintentional pointer scaling (CWE 468)*

Improper mixing of pointer types in an expression may result in references to memory beyond that intended by the program.

This weakness cannot exist in a SPARK program as pointers do not exist in a SPARK.

### *4.1.6 Heap Inspection (CWE 244)*

This occurs when buffers that store sensitive information are freed without being properly cleared. For instance, using `realloc()` to resize buffers can leave the sensitive information in memory, thus exposed to attack.

CWE 244 is a particular example of the more general problem of CWE 226: Sensitive Information Uncleared Before Release. The 'leaks' might occur in main memory or some form of temporary files. For example, a leak could occur via primary memory when data is retained between executing programs. SPARK prevents this because the Examiner will flag uninitialized variables. In other words, an executing SPARK program cannot, for example, declare a large array and then proceed to examine that array for 'interesting' elements (left over from an earlier time).

The case of information leaks via temporary files is not directly ameliorated in a SPARK based system. However, Ada supports the concept of temporary files which are not accessible after the main program completes. An appropriate package would need to be written for SPARK which will give access to the full Ada File_IO package. This is similar to what was done by the implementers of SPARK for Text_IO; i.e., Spark_IO is built on Ada.Text_IO.

### *4.1.7 Null Pointer Dereference (CWE 476)*

A pointer with a value of NULL is used as though it pointed to a valid memory area.

This cannot occur in SPARK. The Java example shows a 'trim' function being applied to a null object which causes "NullPointerException" to be raised. It is important to realize that Java is a heap based system: all 'objects' are obtained from there. Although there are no explicit pointers, the 'handles' can still indicate "no object". This is why the Java Virtual Machine has the NullPointerException. (Perhaps the name of the exception should have been NullObjectException).

The Java code fragment is:

```
String cmd = System.getProperty("cmd");
cmd = cmd.trim();
System.out.println(cmd);
```

the equivalent SPARK code might be:

```
subtype Property_Ix is Integer
        range 1 .. 128;
subtype Property is
        String( Property_Ix );

Cmd : Property :=
Property'( others => ' ' );
-- initialize to blanks

Cmd := Get_Property( "cmd" );
Cmd := Trim( Cmd );
Spark_IO.Put_Line(
Spark_IO.Standard_Output, Cmd, 0 );
```

Cmd is a local variable, not an object allocated from a heap as by System.getProperty in Java. In SPARK, even if the property "cmd" does not exist, the variable Cmd will still have a value: a string of blanks. (Get_Property must return a blank string, or some other well-defined string, for a non extant property). The 'trim' function in this case will do nothing. Hence, no exception will be raised in SPARK. Not wishing to belabor the point, we re-emphasize that the whole concept of SPARK is to have a language such that a program written in it exhibits behavior that is completely determinable statically.

## 4.2 Uncontrolled Format String (CWE 134)

Unfiltered input is used as a string to format data in the printf() style of C/C++ functions.

In SPARK there is no 'format string' as there is no printf-style subprogram. Note that SPARK has formatted I/O; it is built upon Ada's text I/O package (Ada.Text_IO).

## 4.3 Improper Null Termination (CWE 170)

The software does not properly terminate a string with a null character.

This CWE applies only to strings. CWEs 707, 463, 464, or other CWEs refer to general data structures.

The 'String' type in SPARK, previously mentioned in the analysis of CWE 89, is defined as: "...an unconstrained one dimensional array of characters;" viz.,

```
type String is
array (Positive range <>) of Character;
```

'Positive' means the lower bound is 1. Although the type is 'unconstrained', when an object of that type is declared, the bounds must be known by means of a subtype definition. For example if the strings correspond to data entry fields, say in a web application, we might have the following fragment where user IDs are 16 characters long and passwords, 12:

```
subtype id_ix is Integer range 1 .. 16;
subtype pw_ix is Integer range 1 .. 12;
subtype User_Name is String( id_ix );
subtype Password is String( pw_ix);
```

After the type declarations we might declare a user id and password:

```
Uid : User_Name;
Pwd : Password;
```

We could then, for example, make the following assignments, of which two are valid and two invalid. (Each assignment has a comment attached).

```
Uid := "General NIST logon ID";
-- length is 21: invalid
```

The Examiner (or Ada compiler) will detect and flag the above statement. The next one is valid and shows the use of the concatenation operator, '&':

```
Uid := "David" & ' ' & "Jones" & "      ";
--  length is 16: valid
```

Note the use of single quotes (') to delimit a character. Similarly the following assignment is valid:

```
Uid := "Paul Black      ";
--  length is 16: valid
```

Finally, the password assignment is also flagged as invalid:

```
Pwd := "NISTUsr_01";
--  length is 10: invalid.
```

As noted earlier, when a string object is declared, its size must be known. In other words, we are always dealing with fixed length strings. Thus CWE 170 cannot occur because strings in SPARK are of fixed length; terminators are not necessary.

## 4.4 Use of Error-Prone String Functions (CWE 251)

Some string manipulation functions, strcpy() and subcat(), require special, extra checking in code to be used safely with unconstrained input. Such checking is easy to forget, implement incorrectly, or falsely conclude it is not needed.

CWE 251 cannot occur because the only operations on string objects are assignment and concatenation. This is to ensure that the sizes of the string objects are always known statically. If traditional string operations such as 'strlen', 'substr' were desired, one or more packages could be written.

It is necessary to adjust for this dichotomy that is, the static length of strings in SPARK and the dynamic representation in languages such as C and C++, when interfacing.

# 5. Class 2: Weaknesses that Can Be Excluded

In this section we discuss how the SPARK language and toolset work together to prevent CWEs 121, 391 and 457 in programs.

## 5.1 Stack-based Buffer Overflow (CWE 121)

A "buffer overflow" occurs when writing data beyond the fixed memory boundary of a buffer. A stack-based buffer overflow is when the buffer being overwritten is allocated on the stack, for instance, a local variable or a parameter to a function.

While trivial cases like

```
Buffer (11) := -10;
```

will be caught the Examiner or a compiler, since the index expression is static, in general, such expressions may be fully dynamic and impossible to resolve in the Examiner.

We look more closely at CWE 121 to understand why this is not a problem in SPARK. The storage requirements of a SPARK program can be determined statically. This is achieved by forbidding recursion and dynamic arrays. (Note also that pointer types and heap storage are disallowed).

To implement a buffer in SPARK an array type must be used.

A code fragment might be:

```
subtype Index is Integer
              range 1 .. 10;
subtype Sensor_value is Integer
              range -20 .. 60;
type Samples is
     array( Index ) of Sensor_value;
Buffer : Samples;
I : Index;
```

Buffer is bounded; it is impossible to access an element outside the range. A statement such as:

```
Buffer(11) := -10;
```

is immediately detected by the Examiner and so too is:

```
I := 11;
...
Buffer(I) := -10;
```

In this case the assignment to 'I' would be flagged by the Examiner.

If the value of the index is determined by calling a function, such as:

```
I := Some_Complex_Function;
```

In this instance, full analysis and proof for absence of buffer overflows requires the Simplifier to be run on the VCs.

## 5.2 Unchecked Error Condition (CWE 391)

No code exists to handle an error or exception condition which may occur. Ignoring exceptions and other error conditions may allow an attacker to induce unexpected behavior which goes unnoticed.

CWE 391 cannot occur in SPARK for two reasons. First, no exceptions are raised. The SPARK subset of Ada eliminates all predefined exceptions. Second, the Examiner will point out any error conditions that are ignored in the program flow. This is a 'programatic' error, an example being failing to handle a return/status code from a subprogram call. The Examiner insists that the code be used in a meaningful fashion and will flag an error if it is not. It cannot, unlike in other languages, simply be ignored.

## 5.3 Uninitialized Variable (CWE 457)

A variable is created without assigning it a value. It is subsequently referenced in the program, leading to unpredictable or unintended results. In some languages, such as C, an uninitialized variable may contain contents of previously-used memory. An attacker can sometimes read these contents.

CWE 457 is detected by the Examiner in SPARK. All variables must be initialized. However, arbitrary initialization will also be flagged as an error. For example, if a variable is assigned a new value prior to using the initial value, the Examiner will produce an error message indicating that the initial value was not used.

# 6. Class 3: Weaknesses that May Occur

Some weaknesses are at a higher semantic level, for instance, omitted features. Without an independent specification or requirement, there is no way to know whether a feature was mistakenly omitted or the feature should not be in the code.

## 6.1 User Input Weaknesses (CWE 78, 80, 89, 99)

To some extent 78, 80, 89, and 99 are variants. They involve the processing of user input, or 'embedded' user input in the case of 80, and failing to do it properly. Use of SPARK can help reduce, but cannot eliminate, these code weaknesses.

### *6.1.1 OS Command Injection (CWE 78)*

The software uses external input to dynamically construct all or part of a command, which is then passed to the operating system for execution, but the software does not sufficiently enforce which commands and arguments are specified. This could allow attackers to execute unexpected, dangerous commands directly on the operating system. This weakness can lead to a vulnerability in environments in which the attacker does not have direct access to the operating system, such as in web applications. Alternately, if the weakness occurs in a privileged program, it could allow the attacker to specify commands that normally would not be accessible, or to call alternate commands with privileges that the attacker does not have.

There are at least two subtypes of OS command injection:

1. The application intends to execute a single, fixed program that is under its own control. It intends to use externally-supplied inputs as arguments to that program. For example, the program might use system("nslookup HOSTNAME") to run the nslookup command and allow the user to supply a HOSTNAME, which is used as an argument. Attackers cannot prevent nslookup from executing. However, if the program does not remove command separators from the HOSTNAME argument, attackers could supply "localhost; rm -rf *" as input. The semicolon ends the nslookup command, which allows them to remove all files and directories after nslookup has finished executing.
2. The application accepts an input that it uses to fully select which program to run, as well as which commands to use. The application simply redirects this entire command to the operating system. For example, the program might use "exec([COMMAND])" to execute the [COMMAND] that was supplied by the user. If the COMMAND is under attacker control, then the attacker can execute arbitrary commands or programs.

From a weakness standpoint, these variants represent distinct programmer errors. In the first variant, the programmer clearly intends that input from untrusted parties will be part of the arguments in the command to be executed. In the second variant, the programmer does not intend for the command to be accessible to any untrusted party, but the programmer probably has not accounted for alternate ways in which malicious attackers can provide input.

CWE 78 is one of four corresponding to the general problem of 'foreign code'; code that is not part of the SPARK universe. This is a problem simply because the code is not subject to the rigor of SPARK and the error detection possible with the Examiner (see SQL Injection CWE 89).

### *6.1.2 Basic XSS (CWE 80)*

Unfiltered input is passed to a web application that in turn passes that data back to another client. The web application fails to adequately filter user-controlled input and sanitize its own output for any special characters, such as "<", ">", and "&", thus allowing a malicious script to be entered.

CWE 80 is another of four corresponding to the general problem of 'foreign code'; code that is not part of the SPARK universe. As with CWE 78, the code is not subject to the rigor of SPARK and the error detection possible with the Examiner.

### *6.1.3 SQL Injection (CWE 89)*

The application dynamically generates an SQL query based on user input, but it does not sufficiently prevent that input from modifying the intended structure of the query.

Without sufficient removal or quoting of SQL syntax in user-controllable inputs, the generated SQL query can cause those inputs to be interpreted as SQL commands instead of ordinary user data. This can be used to alter query logic to bypass security checks, or to insert additional statements that modify the back-end database.

CWE 89 is another of four corresponding to the general problem of 'foreign code'.

SPARK is a subset of Ada and supports (explicitly) two of its pragmas: Import and Elaborate_Body. **pragma** Import enables a SPARK program to call a subprogram written in another language. Currently, only C, COBOL, and Fortran are defined in the Ada Reference Manual (ARM). Support for interfacing with other languages, such as C++ and Java, are supported by most Ada suppliers.

The general approach is to encapsulate the use of the foreign subprogram (FSP) in a package. The import pragma allows the SPARK code to call the FSP. Data that is being passed to the FSP should be validated as the situation warrants.

For example, in CWEs 78, 80, 89, and 99, the problem is passing dangerous strings along where they can create havoc. Thus these strings need to be validated or sanitized first.

How would SPARK mitigate these problems in the context of CWE 89? As mentioned earlier the first warning is that, to invoke an SQL query, it is necessary to call a non SPARK subprogram. Thus we design a SPARK package to encapsulate this access to an FSP along the following lines:

```
package DB
is
function Valid_Query( SQL_String : in
String ) return Boolean;
procedure Query (
    SQL_String : in String;
    Result : out String );
--# derives Result from SQL_String;
--# pre Valid_Query( SQL_String );
pragma Import (C, Query);
end DB;


package body DB is
function Valid_Query(
     SQL_String : in String )
return Boolean
is
  Apostrophe : constant Character := ''';
  Dash : constant Character := '-';
  Current_Char : Character :=
                           Character'Val(0);
 R_C : Boolean;
begin
-- It will be necessary to scan the
-- string for either valid or invalid
-- characters, depending on what is safer
-- or more efficient.
-- Note that type String is defined in
-- SPARK as an unconstrained one
-- dimensional array of characters; viz.,
--
-- type String is array
--       (Positive range <>) of Character;
--
-- This is a simple screening test for
-- SQL queries, only looking for
-- apostrophe (') and dash (-).
-- Note: Whitelisting, making sure there
-- are only valid characters, is
-- generally safer.
--
-- As written this disallows legal names
-- of the form
-- Rollan-Jones and O'Byrne.
--
-- The production version would probably
-- be more sophisticated.
      for I in Integer
            range SQL_String'Range
      loop
        Current_Char := SQL_String(I);
      exit when Current_Char = Apostrophe
                 or Current_Char = Dash;
      end loop;

      if Current_Char = Apostrophe or
         Current_Char = Dash then
        R_C := False;
      else
        R_C := True;
      end if;

      return R_C;
    end Valid_Query;
  end DB;
```

The package contains two subprograms: one to validate the callers SQL string while the other is a reference to the actual query FSP (via the 'pragma import'). The code fragment to make use of this package might be:

```
-- get input from user, whatever it is
--        Read_Input          (User_String);
-- construct SQL query string from user
-- input Form_Query (User_String,
--                              SQL_String);
-- Check validity of generated query
-- NOTE: If the user forgets to test
-- DB.Valid_Query before caling DB.Query,
-- then the proof of the
-- pre-condition will fail
--
if DB.Valid_Query (SQL_String) then
-- Execute the resulting query
  DB.Query (SQL_String, Result);
else
  Error_Handler;
end if;
```

The definition of `Valid_Query` can be as simple or as complex as the program's requirements dictate. This is more powerful than the kind of "taint" analysis done by other tools. SPARK allows for a completely formal description of exactly what constitutes "validity" for potentially all inputs. Thus, a SPARK interface to an SQL server will encourage a more disciplined approach but is not a panacea for these 'injection' problems.

### *6.1.4 Resource Injection (CWE ID: 99)*

The software allows user-controlled input to control resource identifiers.

CWE 99 is the last of four corresponding to the general problem of 'foreign code'.

## 6.2 Hard-Coded Password (CWE 259)

The software contains a hard-coded password which it uses for its own inbound authentication or for outbound communication to external components.

There are two main variations:

> *Inbound*: the software contains an authentication mechanism that checks for a hard-coded password.
>
> *Outbound*: the software connects to another system or component, and it contains the password for connecting to that component. A better option for both these is to read the password from a configuration or data file.

In the *Inbound* variant, a password is hard-coded into the product and enables some capability. This hard-coded password is the same for each installation of the product, and it usually cannot be changed or disabled by system administrators without manually modifying the program, or otherwise patching the software. If the password is ever discovered or published, then anybody with access to the product can use the capability. Finally, since all installations of the software will have the same password, even across different organizations, this enables massive attacks such as worms to take place.

The *Outbound* variant applies to front-end systems that authenticate with a back-end service. The back-end service may require a fixed password which can be easily discovered. The programmer may simply hard-code those back-end credentials into the front-end software. Any user of that program may be able to extract the password.

CWE 259 cannot be prevented by use of SPARK. This weakness is associated with the development environment and cannot be mitigated by any programming language.

## 6.3 Leftover Debug Code (CWE 489)

Debug code can create unintended entry points in an application.

CWE 489 can be a serious problem. All debug code should be removed. If there is a desire to retain certain special behaviors for system maintenance, etc., said behavior should be handled differently. In the code example given, the 'back door' code can be made secure by the use of SPARK. The 'embedded' invocation is:

```
http://TARGET/authenticate_login.cgi?usern
ame=&password=&debug=1
```

For the problem to occur, the login script, 'authenticate_login.cgi', must have been written as a variadic function; i.e., one with a variable number of arguments. In this case if the optional third parameter, debug, is present, the other two, username and password, are irrelevant. SPARK does not permit variable number of arguments. There would be three parameters: username, password, and mode, and all would have to be present. Defaults are not permitted. The specification of an appropriate SPARK function might appear as:

```
package Authenticate_Login is
   type Mode_T is ( Normal, Debug);
   function Valid_User(
            Username,
            Password : in String;
            Mode     : in Mode_T ) return
   Boolean;
end Authenticate_Login;
```

The body of the function will validate both the user name and the password. If both are valid the next decision is whether the mode is 'normal' or 'debug'; only approved users can operate in the debug mode.

# 7. Class 4: Concurrent Programming Weaknesses (CWEs 367 and 412)

Ada has supported concurrent programming from Ada83 onwards. The subset of Ada that is used by SPARK has been expanded to include some of the concurrent programming features.

## 7.1 Time-of-check Time-of-use race condition (CWE 367)

The software checks the state of a resource before using that resource, but the resource's state can change the check and the use in a way that invalidates the results of the check. This can cause the software to perform invalid actions.

This weakness can be security-relevant when an attacker can influence the state of the resource between check and use. This can happen with shared resources such as files, memory, or even variables in multi-threaded programs.

## 7.2 Unrestricted Critical Resource Lock (CWE 412)

The software properly checks for the existence of a lock on a critical resource, but the lock can be externally controlled or influenced by an actor. This prevents the software from acting on the resource or performing other behaviors that are controlled by the presence of the lock. Relevant locks might include an exclusive lock or mutex. If the lock can be held for an indefinite period of time, then the denial of service could be permanent.

CWEs 367 and 412 represent two of the problems associated with 'concurrent programming': 367 being the need for mutual exclusion and 412 how to implement it safely. They can be reduced by use of RavenSPARK, but not entirely avoided. RavenSPARK is the current version of SPARK from Altran-Praxis. The 'Raven-' part of the name refers to the Ravenscar Profile [5].This profile defines a subset of the Ada tasking model that is deterministic and suitable for static timing analysis. RavenSPARK supports that profile with some additional constraints.

The protected type and protected object (PO) are part of the RavenSPARK definition. In a multitasking environment the PO encapsulates data that is shared by cooperating tasks; it enforces mutual exclusion. Briefly, only one task can be operating on the object at a time; race conditions cannot exist. If another task requires access when the first is manipulating the object, it is blocked. The runtime system implements this. There is no external lock to manipulate and thus CWE 412 is prevented. However, the protected object cannot be a file which is what is shown in the TOCTOU example. Thus CWE 367 is eliminated except for file access and 412 cannot occur while POs are being used. In RavenSPARK, an unprotected but shared variable is absolutely not permitted, so a programmer cannot forget to properly control access to a shared variable.

# 8. Summary

The Table 1 summarizes the findings discussed in the previous sections.

**Table 1. CWE Summary**

| CWE | Class 1 | Class 2 | Class 3 | Class 4 |
|---|---|---|---|---|
| 78 OS Command Injection | | | x | |
| 80 Basic XSS | | | x | |
| 89 SQL injection | | | x | |
| 99 Resource Injection | | | x | |
| 121 Stack-based buffer overflow | | x | | |
| 122 Heap-based Buffer Overflow | x | | | |
| 134 Uncontrolled Format String | x | | | |
| 170 Improper Null Termination | x | | | |
| 244 Failure to Clear Heap Memory Before Release ('Heap Inspection') | x | | | |
| 251 Often Misused: String Management | x | | | |
| 259 Hard-Coded Password | | | x | |
| 367 Time-of-check Time-of-use (TOCTOU) Race Condition | | x | | x |
| 391 Unchecked Error Condition | | x | | |
| 401 Failure to Release Memory Before Removing Last Reference ('Memory Leak') | x | | | |
| 412 Unrestricted Externally Accessible Lock | | x | | x |
| 415 Double Free | x | | | |
| 416 Use After Free | x | | | |
| 457 Use of Uninitialized Variable | | x | | |
| 468 Incorrect Pointer Scaling | x | | | |
| 476 NULL Pointer Dereference | x | | | |
| 489 Leftover Debug Code | | | x | |

In conclusion, CWEs 122, 134, 170, 244, 251, 401, 415, 416, 468, and 476 cannot occur in SPARK. In SPARK, that flavor of CWE 391, referring to raised exceptions cannot occur; that of programatic errors together with CWEs 121 and 457 are detected by the Examiner. CWEs 78, 80, 89, 99, 259, and 489 remain a problem. Under RavenSPARK, CWEs 367 and 412 will not occur for shared data (in protected objects); they can occur for files since they cannot be encapsulated in protected objects.

## 9. ACKNOWLEDGMENTS

Our thanks to NIST for supporting this work.

## 10. REFERENCES


[1] NIST Special Publication 500-268, "Source Code Security Analysis Tool Functional Specification Version 1.0," May 2007.

[2] Common Weakness Enumeration (CWE), http://cwe.mitre.org/.

[3] SPARK GPL Edition, http://libre.adacore.com/libre/tools/spark-gpl-edition/.

[4] Barnes, John, "High Integrity Software: The SPARK Approach to Safety and Security," Addison Wesley, 2006.

[5] ISO/IEC TR 24718:2004 (2004) *Guide for the use of the Ada Ravenscar Profile in high integrity systems.*

[6] Ada Reference Manual with Technical Corrugendum 1 and Ammendment 1, ISO-8652:1995(E) with COR 1: 2000 and Amd 1:2007.

# Enhancing SPARK's Contract Checking Facilities Using Symbolic Execution*

Jason Belt, John Hatcliff, Robby
Kansas State University
belt@ksu.edu, hatcliff@ksu.edu, robby@ksu.edu

David Hardin
Rockwell Collins Advanced Technology Center
dshardin@rockwellcollins.com

Patrice Chalin
Concordia University
chalin@encs.concordia.ca

Xianghua Deng
Google Inc.
wdeng@google.com

## ABSTRACT

SPARK, a subset of Ada for engineering safety and security-critical systems, is one of the best commercially available frameworks for formal-methods-supported development of critical software. SPARK is designed for verification and includes a software contract language for specifying functional properties of procedures. Even though SPARK and its static analysis components are beneficial and easy to use, its contract language is rarely used for stating properties beyond simple constraints on scalar values due to the burdens the associated tool support imposes on developers.

Symbolic execution (SymExe) techniques have made significant strides in automating reasoning about deep semantic properties of source code. However, most work on SymExe has focused on bug-finding and test case generation as opposed to tasks that are more verification-oriented such as contract checking. In previous work we have presented: (a) SymExe techniques for checking software contracts in embedded critical systems, and (b) Bakar Kiasan, a tool that implements these techniques in an integrated development environment for SPARK. In this paper, we give a detailed walk-through of Bakar Kiasan as it is applied to an industrial code base for an embedded security device. We illustrate how Bakar Kiasan provides significant increases in automation, usability, and functionality over existing SPARK contract checking tools, and we present results from performance evaluations of its application to industrial examples.

## Categories and Subject Descriptors

D.2.4 [**Software Engineering**]: Software/Program Verification—*Assertion checkers, Formal methods, Programming by contract, Validation*; D.2.5 [**Software Engineering**]: Testing and Debugging—*Symbolic execution*

*Work supported in part by the US National Science Foundation (NSF) CAREER award 0644288, the US Air Force Office of Scientific Research (AFOSR), Rockwell Collins, and the Natural Sciences and Engineering Research Council (NSERC) of Canada grant 261573.


*SIGAda'11*, November 6–10, 2011, Denver, Colorado, USA.


## General Terms

Algorithms, Reliability, Verification

## Keywords

spark, symbolic execution, program analysis

## 1. INTRODUCTION

The SPARK language and tool framework [2], developed by Altran Praxis and now also marketed and supported by AdaCore, is one of the premier commercial development frameworks for high-assurance software. SPARK is a subset of Ada designed for programming and verifying high assurance applications such as avionics applications certified to DO-178B Level A. It deliberately omits constructs that are difficult to reason about such as dynamically created data structures, pointers, exceptions, and recursion. The SPARK language includes a procedure annotation language for specifying: (a) information flow relationships between procedure parameters and global variables accessed in the procedure, and (b) pre/post-conditions and embedded assertions. The SPARK tool chain has three primary components: the Examiner, Simplifier, and Proof Checker. The Examiner provides standard static analyses for detecting uninitialized variables, dead code, parameter aliasing, and violations of procedure information flow declarations. The Examiner can also generate verification conditions (VCs) for guaranteeing: (a) absence of run-time exceptions (e.g., Ada bounds checking exceptions), and (b) conformance of code to procedure contracts and assertions. The Simplifier is a decision procedure package that processes VCs emitted by the Examiner with the result that they are either discharged (verified) or simplified. The Proof Checker is a proof assistant with very little automation (e.g., no built-in tactics) that can be used to discharge remaining VCs based on arithmetic laws or user-supplied proof rules. SPARK does not include a compiler and can be used with any standard Ada compiler. AdaCore provides one such compiler, the widely used GNAT Pro built on the GCC (GNU Compiler Collection) infrastructure.

SPARK has been used to develop a number of safety/security-critical systems including avionics systems in the Lockheed Martin C130J, EuroFighter Typhoon, and several railway control projects. Currently, an Altran Praxis team of around 60 developers is using SPARK to develop the Interim Future Area Control Tools Support (iFACTS) – a support system for the UK air traffic controllers that will further improve safety and enable controllers to increase the amount of traffic they can comfortably handle. iFACTS is a large safety-critical system with over 150,000 non-comment source lines of code. Our experience with SPARK is derived from its use in security critical projects at Rockwell Collins including the Janus high-speed cryptography engine and several other embedded information assurance devices.

While SPARK is an exemplar of practical application of formal methods in critical applications, most development teams use the Examiner's static analysis capabilities, while the contract checking framework is seldom used. When SPARK contracts are used, they are usually limited to adding simple preconditions necessary to ensure "type safety", *i.e.*, absence of range violations, and this involves stating simple constraints on integers. Contracts were used on the joint Praxis/NSA Tokeneer project to specify constraints on high-level system state transitions, but again these specifications are only simple predicates on enumerated types (representing specific modes that are called out in system requirements). Many industrial applications coded in SPARK manipulate complex data structures. For example, embedded security applications at Rockwell Collins use deeply nested collections of arrays and records *e.g.*, for key storage/manipulation, message and buffer representations, and for message routing. Avionics applications use similar data structures to hold coordinates, way points for navigation, etc. We are unaware of SPARK contracts being used in industrial settings to specify and check correctness properties for these types of program elements. Such contracts would typically include nested quantification over multi-level data structures and significant use of SPARK's array update notation which almost always require intensive manual interaction with SPARK's verification tools.

We believe there are several reasons why industrial development efforts fail to make significant use of the SPARK pre/post-condition notation.

- Many uses of pre/post-conditions (e.g., those that include quantification for reasoning about arrays) will produce VCs that cannot be discharged automatically by SPARK tooling, thus developers must fall back on traditional code inspection or (laborious) manual proof using the SPARK Proof Checker.
- Verification conditions and proof rules necessary for discharging contracts are represented using Functional Description Language (FDL) that is very different from the SPARK programming language. Shifting from source code to a specialized proof language that requires additional training is disruptive to developer workflows.
- Specifying desired functionality as logical expressions in contracts is difficult for complex properties; it is often necessary to introduce "helper" specification functions. In SPARK, the only mechanism to achieve this is to introduce functions without implementations whose behavior is subsequently axiomatized in FDL. Reasoning about these functions usually requires manual interaction with the Proof Checker.
- Although they capture a variety of useful semantic properties, SPARK contracts are not leveraged by other quality assurance (QA) techniques in a manner that would increase the "value proposition" of the framework to developers.

Thus, despite offering a strong formal foundation, the current SPARK contract framework is not realizing its potential due to its requirements of manual interactions, use of unfamiliar languages other than source code, disruptions to workflow, and lack of multiple leverage points. In practice, the above problems often cause projects to avoid using SPARK contracts. For instance, in the research division of Rockwell Collins, even engineers who were quite familiar with formal methods found it more effective to hand-translate SPARK packages to the input language of the Prover tool and check their behavior using Prover model checker. This was how the example presented in Section 2 was originally developed. Even if SPARK contracts were used, such use would most likely be delayed until the late stages of development when they would be introduced and verified by a verification specialist. In either case, the typical SPARK user gets no benefit from the SPARK contract language.

We are building a verification framework called Bakar Kiasan[1] based on *symbolic execution* that significantly enhances the usability of the SPARK contract framework. Though first proposed by King [23] over three and a half decades ago, symbolic execution (SymExe) has experienced a renaissance in recent years as researchers have looked for techniques that automatically discover wide-ranging properties of a program's behavior with little or no developer intervention. Research has centered around using symbolic execution for detection of common faults such as null-pointer de-referencing, buffer overflows, array bounds violations, assertion checking, and test case generation [22, 28, 29, 6]. Much of the work has been carried out in the context of object-oriented languages such as Java [22, 11, 28], C++, and C#.

While SymExe can be applied in many contexts, we are exploring the effectiveness of SymExe in developing and assuring critical systems. Thus, in addition to an emphasis on bug-finding and test-case generation, we also aim to support checking of formal code contracts written in rich specification languages capable of capturing complex functional correctness properties.

We believe that the foundational approach to symbolic execution that we have been pursuing can significantly improve the usability and effectiveness of the SPARK contract language by providing a completely automated bounded verification technology that scales to complex SPARK contracts for industrial code bases. Our aim is not to replace the VCGen framework of SPARK but to complement it by offering highly automated developer-friendly techniques that be used directly in the code(specify)-test(check)-debug(understanding feedback) loop of typical developer workflows. In previous work [4], we described the foundations of our approach and provided a brief description of how our tools could be applied to a portion of the code base of a Rockwell Collins embedded security application. In this paper, we provide a significantly expanded discussion and detailed walkthrough of our tools applied to that example, and we report on additional results for automatically generated unit test suites for complex data structures. Specifically, the contents of this paper include:

- Description of how SPARK contracts can be represented to enable SymExe.
- An overview of the SymExe algorithm and associated bounding strategies used to check SPARK code against our contract representation.
- Presentation of our SymExe tool for SPARK, which in addition to leveraging contracts, includes behavior visualization and test case generation.
- Illustrations of how SymExe provides greater flexibility including the ability to: (a) specify complex behaviors working directly at the source code level as opposed to a separate proof language, (b) forgo conventional compositional checking (as required by SPARK's existing VCGen approach) when methods are not fully specified, and (c) to freely mix logical and executable specifications in SPARK contracts.
- Evaluations that demonstrate significant improvements in the degree of automation required for checking SPARK contracts.

[1] "Bakar" is the word for "spark" in Indonesian, while "Kiasan" is a word meaning "symbolic".

## 2. EXAMPLE

Figure 1 shows excerpts of a SPARK package LinkedSet that provides a representation of a set of Item_Type records. The intention is that the ID field uniquely identifies the record within the set, while the Value holds data (the details of which are irrelevant for this example). This code (minus the contracts) is taken directly from the code base of an embedded security device developed at Rockwell Collins (only variables have been renamed to avoid revealing the nature of the application), and was provided as a challenge problem to the academic authors for demonstrating contract specification/checking capabilities. The academic authors worked with Rockwell Collins engineers to develop what the engineers considered a reasonable approach to contract specification for this example.

The set representation is based on a single-linked list. Since SPARK does not include heap-allocated data, the linked list is implemented using two arrays: (1) Item_List that holds the current elements of the set as well as free slots for elements to be added, and (2) Next_List implements "links" from a set element to another. Used_Head gives the index position in Item_List of the first set item. Similarly, Free_Head marks the index position of the first of the free array elements.

SPARK includes both *procedures* (which may have side-effects) and (side-effect-free) *functions*; we refer to these collectively as *methods*. The parameter passing mechanism is call-by-value-result. Each parameter and global variable referenced by a procedure must be be classified as **in**, **out**, or **in out**. Each method can have a behavioral contract, embedded in Ada comments beginning with a special delimiter character # recognized by the SPARK tools. Procedures can have both **pre** and **post** conditions. The symbol ~ is used (e.g., Item_List~ in the post-condition of Add) to denote the pre-state value of the variable. Instead of post-conditions, functions can have *return constraints*. Method implementations can include *in-line assertions*, which may be used to state loop invariants. The SPARK contract language includes quantifiers and the usual boolean operators .

Since SPARK excludes dynamically-allocated data, all SPARK arrays are allocated statically and must have statically determined bounds (whose sizes are known at compile time). SPARK arrays are values; passing arrays as parameters and assignment between variables of an array type results in an array copy. Arrays can be compared for value equality (structurally) in both method implementations and contracts. In addition, contracts can utilize the array update notation A[I => V] which denotes an array value that is identical to that currently held by array A except that the position given by the expression I maps to the value of the expression V.

There are several representational invariants that are expected to hold for a linked list implemented in this way. For the used and free subsets of the list we expect that: (1) starting from the head of each subset, a terminator is eventually reached, (2) no cycles exist, and (3) the two sets are disjoint and together cover all indices in the underlying array. Additionally it is expected that all the entries contained in the used portion are non-null and have unique id's whereas the elements in the free portion should be null.

In addition to maintaining the above structural invariants, each operation has constraints that should be enforced to characterize their appropriate behavior. The operations return a response code to the user indicating the status of the operation (these are prefixed with DB in the implementation). There are four possible scenarios when attempting to add an entry to the set: (1) the entry already exists (DB_Already_Exists), (2) the set is full (DB_No_Room), (3) the entry is invalid (DB_Input_Check_Fail), or (4) the entry is successfully added to the set (DB_Success). For each of these we expect that the non-null entries contained in the set prior to the operation are still present once the operation completes. Only in the case where the entry is actually added should the set to be modified, and then only by the inclusion of the new entry.

A delete operation will either find and remove the entry with the given id (DB_Success) or indicate that the id was not found (DB_Does_Not_Exist). In either case the entries in the used portion of the set should remain unchanged except for the possible removal of a single entry.

Some of the above constraints are quite simple and natural to express directly in SPARK's contract language. For example, the constraints on DB_Success and DB_Already_Exists for LinkedSet.Add starting at line 186 in Figure 1, even though non-trivial, can be coded using universal/existential quantification as seen in Figure 2. However, almost all the invariant properties listed above would be very difficult to capture using SPARK's first-order logic expressions. A feature of this example that makes the task especially challenging is that fact that in many cases such as in coding up the notion of "reachable", one cannot write the specification directly by quantifying over a single array but instead must follow the *logical* structure given by the Next_List array.

What one really needs is the ability to capture basic notions such as reachability in "helper specifications". To illustrate this we have written the contracts for LinkedSet following this idea as seen in Figure 3. *Unfortunately, in the current SPARK tools, it would be virtually impossible to make any practical use of these contracts.* This is because in the SPARK framework, even though the function bodies above are written in SPARK, the SPARK VCGen verification facilities make no connection between the function implementations and their use in contracts. From the point of view of the SPARK contract verification tools, the bodies of these functions are ignored. The semantics of such functions must instead be specified as axioms (rewrite rules) in the FDL proof language. This adds a considerable level of complexity to developer effort that almost always results contracts not being used.

In contrast, the symbolic execution approach by Bakar Kiasan enables developers to specify the semantics of such functions directly as function implementations in the SPARK programming language – thus, integrating this task directly into developer workflows while avoiding the need for developers to learn a separate specification language (FDL). Figure 3 illustrates how Bakar Kiasan enables the various specification properties introduced above to be coded as "predicates" via SPARK boolean functions.

The function prf_Size computes the number of entries reachable from a given index in Next_List so calling this function with the head of either the free or used subsets will yield the number of entries it contains. To ensure termination, we check that the number of reachable entries is always less than Inf_Length which is simply one more than the length of Item_List. The detection of cycles is performed by prf_Is_Cyclic by ensuring prf_Size never returns Inf_Length. prf_Contains walks over the logical structure of a reachable set using both Item_List and Next_List to determine if a given id is present – something that would be very difficult to do using logical quantification alone. prf_GetItem is similar except it returns the corresponding entry if it is found. prf_Is_Perm checks whether the current elements in the used portion of the set are a permutation of the reachable set which is passed in via its parameters. The property being captured here is that the set should always contain the same entries (using structural equality at line 89) before and after an operation is performed, with the possible exception of a single deleted entry (*i.e.*, Opt_Deleted_ID). prf_Used_Elements_Invariant walks over the used portion of the set ensuring that none of its entries contain null values or ids and

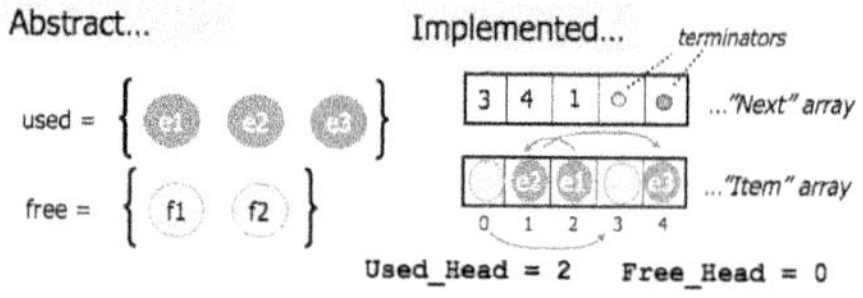

Abstract...

used = { e1 e2 e3 }

free = { f1 f2 }

Implemented...

terminators

| 3 | 4 | 1 | ○ | ● | ..."Next" array

| | e2 | e1 | | e3 | ..."Item" array

0 1 2 3 4

Used_Head = 2 Free_Head = 0

```
-- D a t a   S t r u c t u r e s
type Item_Type is record
  ID    : ID_Type;
  Value : Value_Type;
end record;

Max_Items : constant := 3; -- maximum number of items in set
subtype Index_Type is Word range 0..Max_Items-1;
subtype Link_Type is Word range 0..Max_Items;
type Item_List_Type is array (Index_Type) of Item_Type;
type Next_List_Type is array (Index_Type) of Link_Type;

Next_List : Next_List_Type;
Item_List : Item_List_Type;
Used_Head, Free_Head : Link_Type;

Terminator  : constant := Link_Type'Last;
Inf_Length  : constant := Link_Type'Last + 1;
Null_Item   : constant Item_Type := Item_Type'(Null_ID, Null_Value);
```

```
procedure Get_Value(ID     : in  ID_Type;
                    Value  : out Value_Type;
                    Found  : out Boolean)
  --# global in Item_List, Used_Head, Next_List, Free_Head;
  --# derives Value, Found from ID, Used_Head, Item_List, Next_List &
  --#   null from Free_Head;
  --# pre ID /= Null_ID and then
  --#   prf_Invariant(Next_List, Free_Head, Used_Head, Item_List);
  --# post prf_Invariant(Next_List, Free_Head, Used_Head, Item_List)
  --#   and then prf_Contains(ID, Used_Head, Item_List, Next_List) = Found
  --#   and then (Found -> (Value /= Null_Value))
  --#   and then (not Found -> (Value = Null_Value));
is
  Curr_Index : Link_Type;
begin
  --# accept Flow_Message, 30, Free_Head,
  --#   "Free_Head is only used in call to Invariant";
  Value := Null_Value;
  Curr_Index := Used_Head;
  Found := False;
  while not Found and then Curr_Index /= Terminator loop
    if Item_List (Curr_Index).ID = ID then
      Value := Item_List (Curr_Index).Value;
      Found := True;
    else
      Curr_Index := Next_List (Curr_Index);
    end if;
  end loop;
end Get_Value;
```

```
procedure Add(ID       : in  ID_Type;
              Value    : in  Value_Type;
              Response : out Response_Type)
  --# global in out Item_List, Next_List, Free_Head, Used_Head;
  --# derives Item_List from ID, Value, Item_List, Next_List,
  --#   Free_Head, Used_Head &
  --#   Response, Next_List, Free_Head, Used_Head from
  --#     ID, Item_List, Next_List, Free_Head, Used_Head;
  --# pre (ID /= Null_ID) and then (Value /= Null_Value) and then
  --#   prf_Invariant(Next_List, Free_Head, Used_Head, Item_List);
  --# post prf_Invariant(Next_List, Free_Head, Used_Head, Item_List)
  --#   and then prf_Is_Perm(Next_List~, Used_Head~, Item_List~, Null_ID,
  --#                        Next_List, Used_Head, Item_List)
  --#   and then (Response = DB_No_Room -> (Free_Head~ = Terminator
  --#              and then Free_Head~ = Free_Head))
  --#   and then (Response = DB_Success -> (
  --#     not prf_Contains(ID, Used_Head~, Item_List~, Next_List~)
  --#     and then prf_Contains(ID, Used_Head, Item_List, Next_List)
  --#     and then prf_Size(Used_Head, Next_List) =
  --#              prf_Size(Used_Head~, Next_List~) + 1))
  --#   and then (Response = DB_Already_Exists -> (
  --#     prf_Contains(ID, Used_Head~, Item_List~, Next_List~)
  --#     and then prf_Size(Used_Head, Next_List) =
  --#              prf_Size(Used_Head~, Next_List~)));
is
  Curr_Index : Link_Type;
  Temp_Value : Value_Type;
  Found : Boolean;
begin
  if ID /= Null_ID then
    if Free_Head /= Terminator then
      --# accept Flow_Message, 10, Temp_Value,
      --#   "Assignment to Temp_Value is ineffective";
      Get_Value(ID, Temp_Value, Found);
      --# end accept;
      if not Found then
        Curr_Index := Free_Head;
        Free_Head := Next_List (Free_Head);
        Item_List (Curr_Index).ID := ID;
        Item_List (Curr_Index).Value :=  Value;
        Next_List (Curr_Index) := Used_Head;
        Used_Head := Curr_Index;
        Response := DB_Success;
      else
        Response := DB_Already_Exists;
      end if;
    else
      Response := DB_No_Room;
    end if;
  else
    Response := DB_Input_Check_Fail;
  end if;
  --# accept Flow_Message, 33, Temp_Value,
  --#   "Temp_Value is neither referenced nor exported.";
end Add;
```

```
procedure Delete (ID       : in  ID_Type;
                  Response : out Response_Type)
  --# global in out Item_List, Next_List, Free_Head, Used_Head;
  --# derives Next_List, Free_Head from
  --#   ID, Item_List, Next_List, Free_Head, Used_Head &
  --#   Response, Used_Head, Item_List from
  --#     ID, Item_List, Next_List, Used_Head;
  --# pre (ID /= Null_ID) and then
  --#   prf_Invariant(Next_List, Free_Head, Used_Head, Item_List);
  --# post prf_Invariant(Next_List, Free_Head, Used_Head, Item_List)
  --#   and then prf_Is_Perm(Next_List~, Used_Head~, Item_List~, ID,
  --#                        Next_List, Used_Head, Item_List)
  --#   and then prf_Size(Used_Head, Next_List) <=
  --#            prf_Size(Used_Head~, Next_List~)
  --#   and then ((Response = DB_Does_Not_Exist) <->
  --#     not prf_Contains(ID, Used_Head~, Item_List~, Next_List~))
  --#   and then ((Response = DB_Success) <-> (
  --#     prf_Contains(ID, Used_Head~, Item_List~, Next_List~) and then
  --#     not prf_Contains(ID, Used_Head, Item_List, Next_List)));
is
  Curr_Index : Link_Type;
  Prev_Index : Link_Type;
begin
  Prev_Index := Terminator;
  Curr_Index := Used_Head;
  while Curr_Index /= Terminator and then
        Item_List (Curr_Index).ID /= ID loop
    Prev_Index := Curr_Index;
    Curr_Index := Next_List (Curr_Index);
  end loop;
  if Curr_Index /= Terminator then
    Item_List (Curr_Index) := Null_Item;
    if Prev_Index = Terminator then
      Used_Head := Next_List (Curr_Index);
    else
      Next_List (Prev_Index) := Next_List (Curr_Index);
    end if;
    Next_List (Curr_Index) := Free_Head;
    Free_Head := Curr_Index;
    Response := DB_Success;
  else
    Response := DB_Does_Not_Exist;
  end if;
end Delete;
```

**Figure 1: LinkedSet Example (excerpts)**

```
--#  and then (Response = DB_Success -> (
--#     (for all I in Index_Type => (ID /= Item_List~(I).ID)) and then
--#     (for some I in Index_Type => (ID = Item_List(I).ID))
--#     and then prf_Size(Used_Head, Next_List) =
--#                 prf_Size(Used_Head~, Next_List~) + 1))
```

```
--#  and then (Response = DB_Already_Exists -> (
--#     (for some I in Index_Type =>
--#        (ID = Item_List~(I).ID and then ID = Item_List(I).ID)) and then
--#     and then prf_Size(Used_Head, Next_List) =
--#                 prf_Size(Used_Head~, Next_List~)));
```

**Figure 2: Excerpt of the declarative style of contract for LinkedSet.Add**

```
function prf_Size(head : Link_Type) return Word
  --# global in Next_List;
is
  Cursor : Link_Type;
  Result : Word := 0;
begin
  Cursor := head;
  while Cursor /= Terminator and Result < Inf_Length loop
    Result := Result + 1;
    Cursor := Next_List(Cursor);
  end loop;
  return Result;
end prf_Size;

function prf_Is_Cyclic(head : Link_Type) return Boolean
  --# global in Next_List;
is begin
  return prf_Size(head) = Inf_Length;
end prf_Is_Cyclic;

function prf_Contains(ID : ID_Type) return Boolean
  --# global Used_Head, Item_List, Next_List;
is
  Result : Boolean := False;
  Cursor : Link_Type;
begin
  Cursor := Used_Head;
  while not Result and then Cursor /= Terminator loop
    Result := Item_List(Cursor).ID = ID;
    Cursor := Next_List(Cursor);
  end loop;
  return Result;
end prf_Contains;

function prf_GetItem(ID: ID_Type) return Item_Type
  --# global Used_Head, Item_List, Next_List;
is
  Ret : Item_Type := Null_Item;
  Cursor : Link_Type;
begin
  Cursor := Used_Head;
  while Cursor /= Terminator loop
    if Item_List(Cursor).ID = ID then
      Ret := Item_List(Cursor);
      exit;
    end if;
    Cursor := Next_List(Cursor);
  end loop;
  return Ret;
end prf_GetItem;

function prf_Is_Perm(Old_Next_List   : Next_List_Type;
                     Old_Used_Head   : Link_Type;
                     Old_Item_List   : Item_List_Type;
                     Opt_Deleted_ID  : ID_Type) return Boolean
  --# global Next_List, Used_Head, Item_List;
is
  Result : Boolean := True;
  Old_Item : Item_Type;
  Cursor : Link_Type;
begin
  Cursor := Old_Used_Head;
  while Result and then Cursor /= Terminator loop
    Old_Item := Old_Item_List(Cursor);
    if Old_Item.ID /= Opt_Deleted_ID and then
       Old_Item /= prf_GetItem(Old_Item.ID) then
      Result := False;
    end if;
    Cursor := Old_Next_List(Cursor);
  end loop;
  return Result;
end prf_Is_Perm;

function prf_Used_Elements_Invariant return Boolean
  --# global in Item_List, Next_List, Used_Head;
is
  Cursor, Cursor2 : Link_Type;
  Result : Boolean := True;
begin
  Cursor := Used_Head;
  while Result and then Cursor /= Terminator loop
    Result := Item_List(Cursor).ID /= Null_ID and then
              Item_List(Cursor).Value /= Null_Value;
    Cursor2 := Next_List(Cursor);
    while Result and then Cursor2 /= Terminator loop
      Result := Item_List(Cursor).ID /= Item_List(Cursor2).ID;
      Cursor2 := Next_List(Cursor2);
    end loop;
    Cursor := Next_List(Cursor);
  end loop;
  return Result;
end prf_Used_Elements_Invariant;

function prf_Free_Elements_Invariant return Boolean
  --# global Item_List, Next_List, Free_Head;
is
  Cursor : Link_Type;
  Result : Boolean := True;
begin
  Cursor := Free_Head;
  while Result and then Cursor /= Terminator loop
    Result := Item_List(Cursor).ID = Null_ID and then
              Item_List(Cursor).Value = Null_Value;
    Cursor := Next_List(Cursor);
  end loop;
  return Result;
end prf_Free_Elements_Invariant;

function prf_Invariant return Boolean
  --# global in Next_List, Free_Head, Used_Head, Item_List;
is begin
  return not (prf_Is_Cyclic(Free_Head) or else prf_Is_Cyclic(Used_Head))
    and then prf_Used_Elements_Invariant
    and then prf_Free_Elements_Invariant
    and then prf_Size(Free_Head) + prf_Size(Used_Head) = Max_Items;
end prf_Invariant;
```

**Figure 3: LinkedSet - Contract code (excerpts)**

that each entry has a unique id. prf_Free_Elements_Invariant verifies that the entries which make up the free portion of the set have null values and ids. Finally, prf_Invariant combines several of the previous functions to ensure that the used and free portions of the set are non-cyclic, their respective invariants hold, and their combined size covers all the positions in the array. This function is asserted in both the pre and post conditions for each of the set operations as SPARK does not currently support the concept of a package invariant.

## 3. BAKAR KIASAN SYMBOLIC EXECUTION ENGINE

SymExe characterizes values flowing through a program using logical constraints. Consider the Min example in Figure 4 that returns the minimum of two numbers or 0, whichever is greater. In this case, we are interested in proving that the assertion in line 11 is never executed (i.e., the precondition at line 2 ensure the true-branch in line 10 is infeasible) without knowing specific concrete values. Thus, we introduce special symbolic values $\alpha$ and $\beta$ to act as placeholders for concrete values of A and B, respectively. The computation tree on the right side of Figure 4 illustrates SymExe on the procedure by keeping track of the symbolic values bound to each variable as well as logical constraints (*i.e.*, the *path condition* given in curly brackets {..}).

Initially, the constraint set is empty because we know nothing about $\alpha$ and $\beta$. The precondition at line 2 asserts the constraints that must hold on these values upon entering Min so $\alpha \geq 0$ and $\beta \geq 0$ are assumed to hold (i.e., the cases where $\alpha < 0$ and/or $\beta < 0$ are considered infeasible). After executing line 6, we know that Z=$\alpha$, thus, (A=$\alpha$ and B=$\beta$ and Z=$\alpha$). At line 7, both the condition ($\beta < \alpha$) and its negation ($\beta \geq \alpha$) are satisfiable (i.e., there are integer values for $\alpha$ and $\beta$ that satisfy these conditions), consider both program executions following the conditional's true-branch and its false-branch; thus, the initial path on the right side of the figure splits into two possible cases. At line 10, the program state is characterized by either (A=$\alpha$ and B=$\beta$ and Z=$\beta$ and $\beta < \alpha$) or

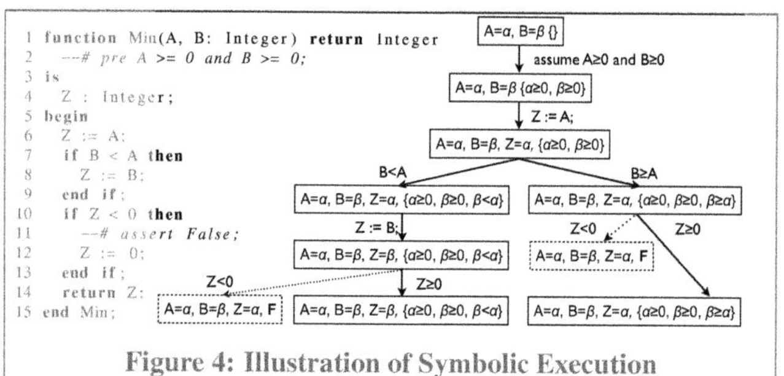


**Figure 4: Illustration of Symbolic Execution**

(A=$\alpha$ and B=$\beta$ and Z=$\alpha$ and $\beta \geq \alpha$). The constraints imply that the if-condition at line 10 is false in either situation (as indicated by the F for the path condition for the "true" cases) – there is no *feasible path* (no possible assignment of concrete values to inputs) that lead to line 11—and thus exploration along these paths is ignored.

Bakar Kiasan includes an interface to underlying decision procedures (including CVC3 [3], Yikes [13], and Z3 [10]). These are used to determine if constraints in path conditions are satisfiable in order to make decisions at branching points such as the ones at lines 5 and 8, and more generally, to determine if boolean conditions in method contracts are satisfiable. Constraints to be passed to conventional decision procedures are first passed through Kiasan's Lightweight Decision Procedure (LDP) module [5]. LDP contains a collection of rules for rapid solving of common constraint shapes and for implementing various forms of constant propagation that allow many constraints to be solved without the overhead of pushing constraints all the way out to an external decision procedure. It has been demonstrated that LDP can give a significant reduction in analysis time (by an order of magnitude) [5]. For SPARK scalar types, Bakar Kiasan depends on LDP and the underlying decision procedures for constraint solving. Developing SymExe to better support dynamically-allocated objects [22, 29, 11] has been a significant focus of previous research. Since SPARK uses only statically-allocated and value-based composite structures (array/records), previous approaches need to be adapted to this setting.

In contrast to other approaches, however, Bakar Kiasan supports *both* logical and graph-based symbolic representations of complex structures. In the logical representation, Bakar Kiasan uses supported theories in underlying decision procedures for representing values of arrays and records. In the graph-based representation, Kiasan uses an adaptation of [11] in which an explicit-state representation (similar to what would be used in explicit-state model checking) is used to model composite structures, and decision procedure support is used only to handle constraints on scalar values. Our approach for Java is adapted for SPARK by optimizing away aliasing cases, and it is enhanced to handle value-based structures instead of reference-based structures by using an optimized form of copy-on-write state tree structures.

The symbolic value manipulation above is incorporated in a depth-first exploration. Since SymExe does not merge state information at program joint points after branches and loops, the analysis may not terminate when the program being checked contains loops or recursion, unless inductive predicates such as loop invariants are provided at these loops and recursion points, as shown by [18]. However, in the context of programs manipulating complex structures, precise loop invariants are difficult to obtain.

A key goal of Bakar Kiasan is to offer developers an approach that provides meaningful checking without requiring the effort of writing loop invariants. The usual approach to address the termination issue is to employ some form of bounding. There are a variety of bounding mechanisms that have been used in the literature, such as loop bounding, depth bounding (*i.e.*, limiting the number of execution steps), bounding on the length of method call chains, etc. The use of these bounding mechanisms leads to an under-approximation of program behaviors. Technically, this means that the analysis is unsound in general, and care must be taken when interpreting analysis reports that indicate no bugs are found (errors may exist in the portion of the program's state space that was not explored). To compensate, Bakar Kiasan notifies users when a bound is exhausted with the program point (and state) where it occurs, thus, users are warned of potential behaviors that are not analyzed.

These are trade-offs that we are certainly willing to accept. The under-approximation and path splitting means that the analysis yields no false positives. Moreover, the analysis will provide complete verification when the procedure includes no loops (as often occurs in embedded programs). Most importantly, as we will explore in the following section, it allows developers to easily check sophisticated properties that, in practice, they would never check using totally automatic non-bounded methods.

# 4. CHECKING SPARK CONTRACTS IN BAKAR KIASAN

Most contract checking tools work compositionally and require that every method be given a contract. Bakar Kiasan provides greater flexibility by providing the ability to check SPARK program behaviors either compositionally, non-compositionally, or mixed. Intuitively, when analyzing a procedure $P$, Kiasan starts by *assuming* $P$'s pre-condition (*i.e.*, adding the pre-condition to the path condition as a conjunct). The analysis proceeds by symbolically executing $P$'s body, and then *asserting* $P$'s post-condition (*i.e.*, branching into two paths; one assumes the post-condition, and the other assumes the negation of the post-condition that leads to an error state). If $P$ calls another procedure $Q$, Kiasan can symbolically execute $Q$ directly (non-compositional), or substitute $Q$ by its contract (compositional, via translation of contracts to executable form described below), as instructed by the user.

When applying non-compositional checking to $Q$, Kiasan *asserts* $Q$'s pre-condition, performs appropriate parameter passing mechanics, and continues on with its depth-first exploration. Kiasan *asserts* $Q$'s post-condition when it is encountered along each explored path. When applying compositional checking to $Q$, Kiasan *asserts* $Q$'s pre-condition, havocs (i.e., assigns fresh unconstrained symbolic values to) all $Q$'s **out** variables, and then *assumes* $Q$'s post-condition. These steps ensure that $Q$'s effect on **out** variables as specified by its contract is captured by: (a) starting with no knowledge about the variables' values, and then (b) applying the constraints in $Q$'s post-condition which would typically constrain the values of the **out** variables. If no contract is supplied for a procedure, the procedure is treated as if its pre/post-condition expressions are both **true** (*i.e.*, checking always succeeds but the values of **out** variables are unconstrained).

Kiasan processes contracts by (automatically) translating each contract to an executable representation in the SPARK programming language that can be processed using the same interpretive engine used to process SPARK procedure implementations. Since SPARK's contract language is a super set of the expression language of its programming language, many aspects of this translation process are achieved rather directly. In the following paragraphs, we describe how we obtain an executable representation for additional elements of the contract language.

An "old" expression (i.e., $e$~, for an expression $e$) in the post-condition of procedure $P$ is handled via transformation. Intuitively,

$e$'s value is saved to a (fresh) variable $x$ before $P$ is executed, and upon post-condition checking, $e\sim$ is replaced with $x$. This strategy applies both to SPARK scalar and complex structure (array and record) values (recall that SPARK has a value semantics for complex structures). In addition, since SPARK's contract expression language is side-effect free, several occurrences of $e\sim$ can be substituted with the same variable. Old expression processing is illustrated for the Inc procedure below; the code on the left hand side is transformed by Kiasan into the one in the right hand side:

```
procedure Inc(I: in out Integer)...            begin
  --# pre  I > 0;                                 assume I > 0;
  --# post I = I~ + 1;                            oldI := I;
is                                                I := I+1;
begin                                             assert I = oldI + 1;
   I := I+1;                                   end Inc;
end Inc;
```

Since SPARK records and arrays are value-based, the contract language provides an equality operation (=) that can be used to test entire records and arrays for equality regardless of their level of complexity/nesting. In Kiasan's logical representation of arrays/records, there is a fairly direct translation to the equality operators and function update notation used by underlying decision procedures. In the graph-based arrays/records symbolic mode, Kiasan uses its own optimized algorithm tailored specifically for checking SPARK value-based arrays and records adapted from [11].

Kiasan transforms quantifications into loops. Universal and existential quantification of the forms for all $x$ in $\tau$ => $\phi(x)$ and for some $x$ in $\tau$ => $\phi(x)$, respectively, are transformed as illustrated below (using a pseudo-code notation to capture the intuition):

```
-- universal                          -- existential
Result := True;                       Result := False;
S := KiasanValues(τ);                 S := KiasanValues(τ);
for x in S loop                       for x in S loop
 if not φ(x) then                       if φ(x) then
    Result := False;                       Result := true;
    exit;                                  exit;
  end if;                                end if;
end loop;                             end loop;
```

Using this transformation scheme, nested quantifications become nested loops. Use of the Kiasan function KiasanValues allows the analysis to be configured to implement different exploration strategies for the array elements. In its simplest form, the function simply returns all elements of the range specified by $\tau$. Executing the loop body implementing the quantification may lead to Kiasan's loop bound being exhausted if the number of array elements exceeds the loop bound. To work around this issue, users can configure Kiasan to return a bounded number of distinct and ordered (*i.e.*, strictly ordered) fresh symbolic (or concrete) values in $\tau$, with the hope that these values would act as witnesses to uncover inconsistency between the program and its specification. Regardless, Kiasan warns the users if there are potential behaviors that are not analyzed (*i.e.*, potentially unsound). We adopt this pragmatic approach for the sake of giving users some helpful feedback due to the inherent limitation (i.e., incompleteness) of decision procedures on general quantifications.

# 5. BAKAR KIASAN METHODOLOGY AND TOOLS

Developers can interact with Bakar Kiasan in two ways: (1) via the command line interface for which a comprehensive HTML report is generated as seen in Figure 5 and (2) via GUI built as an Eclipse plug-in as seen in Figure 7. The GUI, which is integrated with both AdaCore's GNATBench and the Hibachi Eclipse plugins, provides the ability to invoke the AdaCore GNAT compiler and SPARK tools, and visualize typical Eclipse error mark-ups corresponding to errors reported by the compiler and SPARK tools. Below, we give a brief overview of Bakar Kiasan capabilities that directly impact developer workflows and the methodology of the tool.

**Coverage information:** Gaining an appropriate understanding of what portions of a program's behavior have been explored or omitted is an important methodological aspect of applying bounded verification. To aid in this, both the Kiasan HTML report and GUI provide extensive branch and statement coverage information that allow developers to see the portions of the code that were unexplored, either due to the program's logic or as a result of bound exhaustion.

For example, Figure 5 shows Kiasan's coverage information for LinkedSet.Add. The **Statistics for methods called** panel shows that full coverage for Add was not obtained (94% for statements and 83% for branches)[2]. Referring to the **Source Code** panel it can be seen that the false branch of the conditional at line 225 was never explored which is due to the pre-condition asserting ID /= Null_ID at line 179 in Figure 1. In this case the developer would likely chose to weaken the pre-condition in order to achieve 100% coverage as checking for null input is a good defensive programming technique.

In regards to bound exhaustion, the coverage information typically drives an iterative process where contracts/code are debugged using smaller bounds and then bounds are increased to obtain desired levels of coverage. It is important to note that Kiasan gives an exhaustive (*i.e.*, *complete* in a technical sense) exploration of program behavior within bounds (relative to limitations of decision procedures such as non-linear arithmetic). The factor limiting coverage is not precision of the analysis (*e.g.*, within analysis bounds, Kiasan always gives 100% MCDC coverage of reachable code), it is rather the required analysis time.

**Visualizing procedure inputs/outputs and constraints:** Gaining intuition and a proper understanding of a procedure's input and output behavior is an important element of writing and debugging contracts. To assist in this, for each path explored in a contract/procedure, Kiasan generates a *use case visualization* that provides an example of a concrete pre/post-state for that path. These use cases are constructed by calling model finders that are usually part of decision procedures such as Yices and Z3 to find a solution to the symbolic pre/post-state constraints for the path.

For example, the **Test Cases** panel in Figure 5 presents a portion of the sixteen use cases that were generated for LinkedSet.Add for a set of size 3. Figure 6 shows the detailed view of the fourth use case corresponding to a path through the method where an entry is successfully added. The pre-state shows the element to be added has ID=3 and Value=1. Index position 1 of the Item_List holds a null entry, and the post-state shows the newly added item replacing this entry. The index 3 is the terminator for this example, thus the post-state with Free_Head=3 indicates that the "free list" is now empty.

Figure 7 shows the GUI view of the second generated use case for LinkedSet.Delete which corresponds to the successful deletion of an entry with ID=0 from a full set (*i.e.*Free_Head=3). The pre-state shows the corresponding entry is at index position 0 which is replaced with a null entry in the post-state and the index is moved to the "free list" (Free_Head=0).

[2]Kiasan relies on the Examiner to perform flow analysis and therefore skips the **accept** contract statements at lines 202 and 205 and does not included them in the coverage statistics.

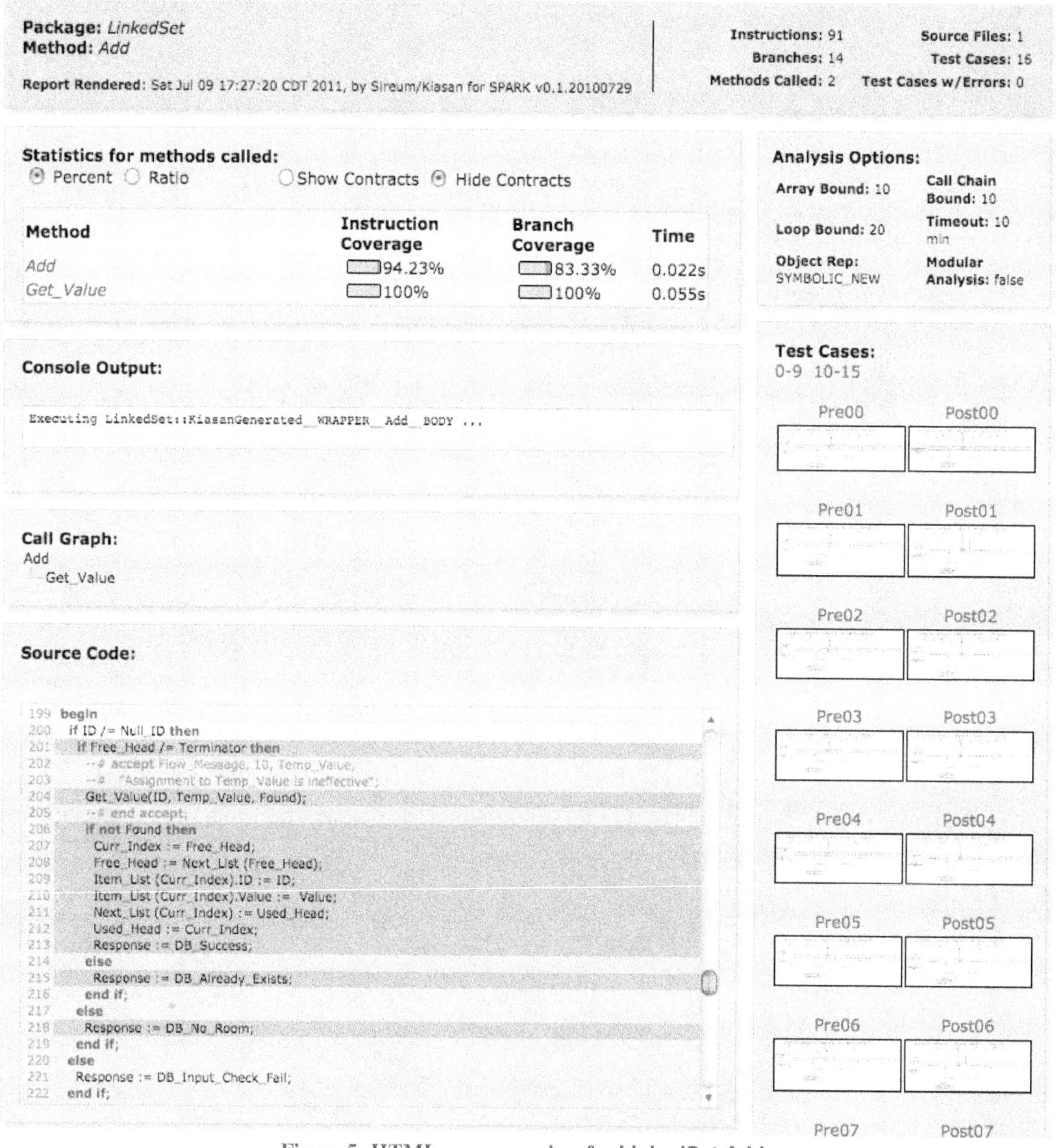

**Package:** *LinkedSet*
**Method:** *Add*

**Report Rendered:** Sat Jul 09 17:27:20 CDT 2011, by Sireum/Kiasan for SPARK v0.1.20100729

**Instructions:** 91
**Branches:** 14
**Methods Called:** 2

**Source Files:** 1
**Test Cases:** 16
**Test Cases w/Errors:** 0

**Statistics for methods called:**

Percent Ratio Show Contracts Hide Contracts

| Method | Instruction Coverage | Branch Coverage | Time |
|---|---|---|---|
| *Add* | 94.23% | 83.33% | 0.022s |
| *Get_Value* | 100% | 100% | 0.055s |

**Console Output:**

```
Executing LinkedSet::KiasanGenerated__WRAPPER__Add__BODY ...
```

**Call Graph:**

Add
Get_Value

**Source Code:**

```
begin
  if ID /= Null_ID then
    if Free_Head /= Terminator then
      --# accept Flow_Message, 10, Temp_Value,
      --#   "Assignment to Temp_Value is ineffective";
      Get_Value(ID, Temp_Value, Found);
      --# end accept;
      if not Found then
        Curr_Index := Free_Head;
        Free_Head := Next_List (Free_Head);
        Item_List (Curr_Index).ID := ID;
        Item_List (Curr_Index).Value := Value;
        Next_List (Curr_Index) := Used_Head;
        Used_Head := Curr_Index;
        Response := DB_Success;
      else
        Response := DB_Already_Exists;
      end if;
    else
      Response := DB_No_Room;
    end if;
  else
    Response := DB_Input_Check_Fail;
  end if;
```

**Analysis Options:**

**Array Bound:** 10
**Call Chain Bound:** 10
**Loop Bound:** 20
**Timeout:** 10 min
**Object Rep:** SYMBOLIC_NEW
**Modular Analysis:** false

**Test Cases:**
0-9 10-15

Pre00 Post00
Pre01 Post01
Pre02 Post02
Pre03 Post03
Pre04 Post04
Pre05 Post05
Pre06 Post06
Pre07 Post07

Figure 5: HTML summary view for LinkedSet.Add

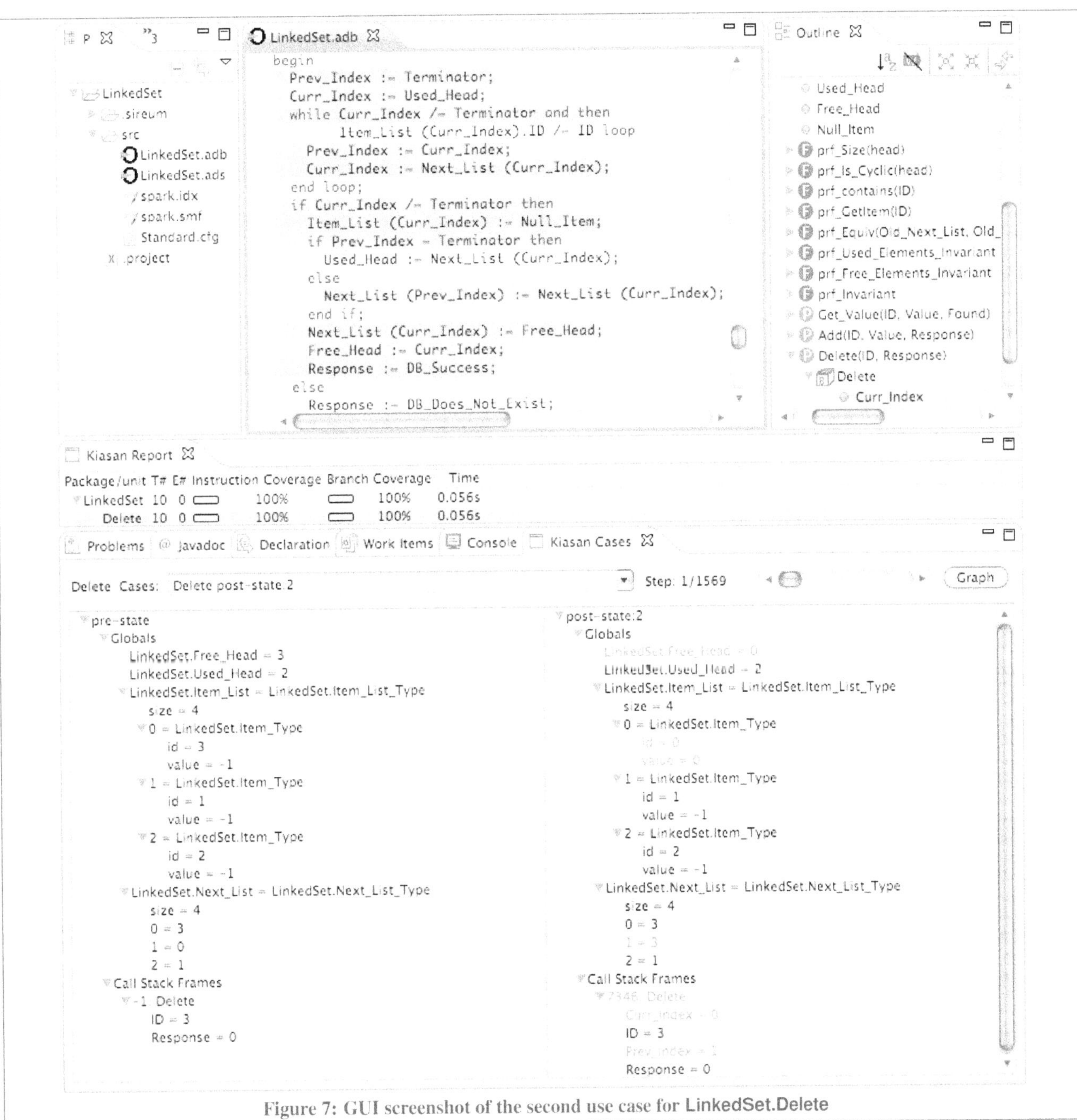


Figure 7: GUI screenshot of the second use case for LinkedSet.Delete

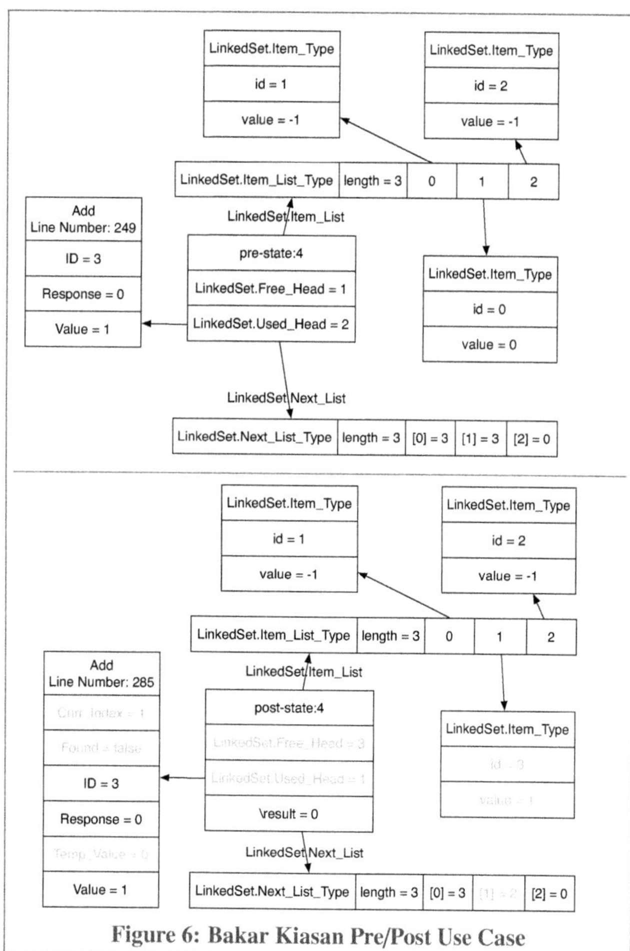


**Figure 6: Bakar Kiasan Pre/Post Use Case**

Although these examples are taken from a procedure with a contract, the use case visualizations are also useful when applied to procedures before contracts are written to help understand input/output relationships and guide the developer in writing contracts. In the GUI, developers can also step through the statements along each path in the use case and see both concrete values and symbolic constraints at each step.

**Test case generation:** SymExe is widely used for test case generation, and the same techniques can be applied here to generate a test in the AUnit format using the concrete values provided in the use cases. Although the application of Kiasan already "checks the code" and no additional bugs would be uncovered by running the generated tests, we have found that generation of test cases can provide additional confidence to people unfamiliar with formal methods because they provide evidence external to the tool using quality assurance concepts that they are well acquainted with (*i.e.*, testing) that Kiasan is correctly exploring the program's state-space.

Care must be taken when generating such test cases to ensure that they obey the semantics of the program. For example, the array based data structures that are being referenced for LinkedSet are declared in the package implementation and are therefore not visible to external packages. Techniques such as reflection are typically employed when similar issues are encountered while generating test cases in other programming languages, however Ada does not support such functionality. To work around this, Kiasan's test case generation creates a modified version of the program in which the package's API is enhanced by adding helper methods which can read and/or write to the private data structures.

```
package body LinkedSet is
  ...
  procedure Add_4_pre_initialialization is begin
    Free_Head := 1;
    Used_Head := 2;
    Item_List := Item_List_Type'(
      0 => Item_Type'(id => 1, value => -1),
      1 => Item_Type'(id => 0, value => 0),
      2 => Item_Type'(id => 2, value => -1));
    Next_List :=
      Next_List_Type'(0 => 3, 1 => 3, 2 => 0);
  end Add_4_pre_initialialization;


  function Add_4_post_check return Boolean is begin
    return (Free_Head = 3)
      and then (Used_Head = 1)
      and then (Item_List = Item_List_Type'(
          0 => Item_Type'(id => 1, value => -1),
          1 => Item_Type'(id => 3, value => 1),
          2 => Item_Type'(id => 2, value => -1)))
      and then (Next_List =
        Next_List_Type'(0 => 3, 1 => 2, 2 => 0));
  end Add_4_post_check;
  ...
end LinkedSet;
```

```
package body LinkedSet_TestSuite is
  ...
  procedure Add_4_Test_Case(R : in out AUnit.Test_Cases.Test_Case'Class) is
    Response_OUT : LinkedSet.Response_Type;
  begin
    LinkedSet.Add_4_pre_initialization;

    LinkedSet.Add(ID => 3, Value => 1, Response => Response_OUT);

    Assert(Response_OUT = 0 and then LinkedSet.Add_4_post_check);
  end Add_4_Test_Case;
  ...
end LinkedSet_TestSuite;
```

**Figure 8: Excerpt of generated AUnit code for LinkedSet.Add**

Figure 8 shows the generated AUnit test case for the LinkedSet.Add use case detailed in Figure 6. The AUnit procedure LinkedSet_TestSuite.Add_4_Test_Case first calls the embedded procedure LinkedSet.Add_4_pre_initialization which initialize the data structures to the values prescribed by the use case. It then makes the actual call to LinkedSet.Add with the arguments ID=3 and Value=1. Finally, it verifies the operation was a success (Response_OUT = 0) and calls LinkedSet.Add_4_post_check to ensure that the actual post-state values of LinkedSet's data structures match the expected results generated by Kiasan. As can be seen, the language features of Ada (*e.g.*, array/record aggregate notation and structural based equality operators for composite data structures) makes the translation from the use cases to actual test cases very straight foward.

We now turn to key novel features of Bakar Kiasan that dramatically improve the usefulness of the SPARK contract language.

**No loop invariants required:** The existing SPARK tool chain and other VCGen techniques that only aim for complete verification require loop invariants. While progress has been made on research for inferring invariants [25, 7], these techniques typically do not perform very well when complex data structures are involved. For example, consider the loop in Get_Value of Figure 1. An invariant for this loop would be very difficult for a developer to write using the logical expressions of SPARK's contract language because the loop is not iterating directly over the array (sequential progression through indices), but rather over the logical structure of the "used list" which jumps back and forth among index positions of the Item_List array via indirection realized by index values held in the Next_List. We believe that it is unlikely that a typical developer would *ever* use the existing SPARK tools to check this contract/procedure. Insisting on the presence of loop invariants before providing any sort of conclusive information is a serious impediment to the practical use of contracts. In contrast, Kiasan checks this contract without loop invariants automatically. Even though Kiasan requires relatively small bounds to be tractable, this gives a very thorough analysis of the structure of the code/contract.

**Blended logical/executable contracts:** SPARK provides a contract language based on first order logic. Functional abstraction is currently not supported in the contract language itself, thus there is no way to define "subcontracts" or "lemmas" that can be referenced in other contracts. As discussed earlier, SPARK only provides a limited mechanism whereby "proof functions" are declared and used within a contract, where the semantics of proof functions is specified in the SPARK FDL proof language. From the point of view of tool engineering, a benefit of the symbolic execution approach is that it uses a uniform mechanism to interpret contracts and code. Thus, it enables us to move beyond the capabilities of the existing SPARK tools to allow contracts in which "declarative" first-order logic based specifications are freely mixed with "executable" specifications. This is best illustrated in the example of Figure 1 by the ability to define the semantics of the rather complex data structure invariants with relatively straightforward executable functions in Figure 3. Since all functions are guaranteed to be side-effect free in SPARK, this feature allows one to express complex properties (e.g., the prf_Contains function of Figure 3) in a form that is simpler and familiar to developers. We have found this capability to be extremely useful in practice. Ultimately, we envision a methodology which would gracefully move toward full functional verification by enabling the executable semantics of the helper functions to be incrementally switched out and replaced by corresponding definitions in an interactive theorem prover.

In our experience, due to the manner in which Kiasan's algorithm handles symbolic array indices in declarative specifications, executable contracts can sometimes yield verification performance advantages. Thus, the executable style of contracts can be used to write "optimized" contracts. For example, instead of the executable style of specification used in Figure 1, Figure 2 shows how a portion of the LinkedSet.Add contract could be refactored to use a more declarative style of specification using quantification over the linked set's array representations. When considering how Kiasan's contract checking proceeds on this example, up to the point where the quantification is processed, Kiasan stores only symbolic values for the indices of two arrays. This provides an efficient means of representing the contract/procedure's state-space – a given set of symbolic indices for a particular path may represent hundreds of unique concrete sets. Recall from Section 4 that Kiasan transforms quantifications into loops that iterate over each element from KiasanValues. For LinkedSet this defaults to the range defined by LinkedSet.Index_Type which is a concrete set containing {0,1,2} when LinkedSet.Max_Items=3. Unfortunately, the use of quantification at this point will cause Kiasan to consider all the possible ways of mapping these concrete values to the symbolic indices it is maintaining, thus forcing it to explore all of the concrete paths through the procedure. In contrast, the executable representation follows the logical structure of the linked set and enables array indices to be symbolic deeper into the analysis before they must be exhaustively instantiated with concrete values.

**Compositional/Non-compositional checking:** Most VCGen approaches including the one used by the SPARK tools requires contract checking to proceed compositionally. That is, when the implementation of a procedure $P$ calls another procedure $Q$, the analysis of $P$ does not examine $Q$'s implementation but instead only examines $Q$'s contract, which in essence, provides a summary of $Q$'s behavior. The advantage of compositional checking is that it is quite scalable and modular since each procedure can be processed independently without requiring a whole-program analysis. The disadvantage of a purely compositional approach is that it requires that all procedures/functions have contracts. While Kiasan works in a compositional manner as explained in Section 4, it can also support non-compositional checking. Specifically, in situations where a developer omits a contract for a procedure $Q$, when processing a call to $Q$, Kiasan will "dive down" into the implementation of $Q$ and use the implementation instead of a contract to generate the symbolic states representing the $Q$'s behavior. This ability to support non-compositional reasoning makes it easier for developers to start benefiting from contracts. Contracts can be specified for the most important methods and omitted for the rest.

**Bounded checking matching well with SPARK applications:** The style of bounded checking, while technically not providing the complete checking of VCGen/theorem-prover frameworks, in practice, it often completes the verification of procedures in embedded applications because such applications often have procedures without loops. In addition, embedded applications usually statically bound the size of data structures—which is a requirement in SPARK. Compared to conventional applications, this increases the likelihood that significant portions of a program's state-space can be covered within the bounding employed by Kiasan.

# 6. EVALUATION

In this section, we report on the effectiveness of Bakar Kiasan when applied to a collection of examples representative of code found in embedded information assurance applications . Information about individual methods from these examples is displayed in Table 1. The sorting examples are a collection of library methods that manipulate array-based data structures as might be used to maintain configurable rules for managing message processing. **IntegerSet** and **LinkedSet** are representative of data structures used to maintain data packet filtering and transformation. **IntegerSet** provides an array-based implementation of an integer set data structure that adds an element by inserting it at the end of the occupied slots in the array and deletes an element by sliding the contents of occupied slots at higher index positions down one slot to reclaim the slot at which the element was deleted. **LinkedSet**[3], described earlier in Section 2, comes directly from a Rockwell Collins code base and uses two arrays to provide a set implementation with more efficient additions/deletions. The MMR (MILS Message Router) is an idealized version of a MILS infrastructure component (first proposed by researchers at the University of Idaho [26]) designed to mediate communication between partitions in a *separation kernel* [27]—the foundation of specialized real-time platforms used in security contexts to provide strong data and temporal separation. The MMR example is especially challenging to reason about because messages flow through a shared pool of memory slots (represented as one large array) where the partition "ownership" of slot contents changes dynamically and is maintained indirectly via two other two-dimensional arrays that hold indices into the memory array.

For each of these examples, **C-LoC** and **I-LoC** in Table 1 gives the number of lines of code in the method contract and implementation, respectively, broken down as $X/Y$ where $X$ is the LoC appearing directly in the contract or implementation and $Y$ is the LoC appearing in helper functions. For **Helper** $X/Y$, $X$ is the number of helper functions used in the contract; $Y$ is the number of methods called in the implementation.

We seek to answer two primary questions with this evaluation: **Question (I):** can Bakar Kiasan provide a significant increase over

[3]LinkedSet.Add_Declarative is the refactored version of Add from Figure 2 in which quantification is used the post-condition

| Package.Procedure Name | C-LoC | I-LoC | Helper | Loop | VC | k=3 | k=4 | k=5 | k=6 | k=7 | k=8 |
|---|---|---|---|---|---|---|---|---|---|---|---|
| Sort.Bubble | 1/23 | 14/4 | 3/1 | 2 | 13/18 | 0.17 | 0.96 | 2.09 | 8.43 | 71.72 | 890.18 |
| Sort.Insertion | 1/21 | 11/0 | 3/0 | 2 | 10/14 | 0.15 | 0.98 | 2.06 | 8.24 | 70.72 | 892.17 |
| Sort.Selection | 1/21 | 15/0 | 3/0 | 2 | 28/30 | 0.16 | 1.06 | 2.28 | 9.95 | 90.14 | 1356.18 |
| Sort.Shell | 1/21 | 15/0 | 3/0 | 3 | 17/18 | 0.15 | 0.98 | 2.12 | 8.47 | 74.09 | 941.99 |
| IntegerSet.Get_Element_Index | 7/0 | 8/0 | 0/0 | 1 | 8/11 | 0.04 | 0.05 | 0.06 | 0.07 | 0.08 | 0.10 |
| IntegerSet.Add | 8/29 | 4/2 | 4/3 | 0 | 3/5 | 0.24 | 0.44 | 0.62 | 0.79 | 0.80 | 1.04 |
| IntegerSet.Remove | 8/27 | 6/0 | 4/1 | 0 | 5/6 | 0.16 | 0.30 | 0.56 | 0.96 | 1.21 | 1.36 |
| IntegerSet.Empty | 1/0 | 2/0 | 0/0 | 0 | 3/3 | 0.02 | 0.02 | 0.02 | 0.02 | 0.02 | 0.02 |
| LinkedSet.Get_Value | 6/45 | 12/0 | 6/0 | 1 | 9/10 | 0.64 | 0.88 | 1.13 | 1.51 | 2.19 | 2.85 |
| LinkedSet.Add | 15/51 | 23/12 | 6/1 | 0 | 14/16 | 0.48 | 0.72 | 1.01 | 1.47 | 2.17 | 3.02 |
| LinkedSet.Add_Declarative | 15/51 | 23/12 | 6/1 | 0 | 14/16 | 0.43 | 0.73 | 1.66 | 5.26 | 34.96 | 379.34 |
| LinkedSet.Delete | 14/45 | 22/0 | 6/0 | 1 | 18/21 | 0.52 | 0.72 | 1.03 | 1.56 | 2.10 | 2.75 |
| LinkedSet.Init | 1/37 | 10/0 | 5/0 | 2 | 16/17 | 0.05 | 0.04 | 0.04 | 0.05 | 0.05 | 0.05 |
| MMR.Fill_Mem_Row | 3/1 | 6/1 | 0/1 | 1 | 8/10 | 0.18 | | | | | |
| MMR.Zero_Mem_Row | 5/1 | 3/1 | 0/1 | 1 | 6/7 | 0.19 | | | | | |
| MMR.Zero_Flags | 4/0 | 3/0 | 0/0 | 1 | 6/7 | 0.05 | | | | | |
| MMR.Read_Msgs | 15/63 | 5/13 | 6/5 | 0 | 3/4 | 1.71 | | | | | |
| MMR.Send_Msg | 10/24 | 6/1 | 3/3 | 0 | 4/5 | 0.50 | | | | | |
| MMR.Route | 22/82 | 22/1 | 9/2 | 2 | 62/67 | 13.90 | | | | | |

**Table 1: Experiment Data (excerpts)**

the existing SPARK tool chain VCGen approach in the level of automation of contract checking? and **Question (II):** is the time required for Kiasan contract checking short enough to allow the tool to be employed as part of the developer code/test/debug cycles?

Regarding **Question (I)**, there are at least three forms of manual activity required to use the SPARK contract checking framework that go beyond what is required by Bakar Kiasan: (1) the need to supply loop invariants, (2) the need to add axioms to provide the semantics for uninterpreted functions used in contracts, and (3) the need to manually discharge VCs that are left unproven by the SPARK tools (we refer to these as "undischarged VCs").

**Loop invariants:** The **Loop** column records the number of loops in the implementation and indicates that well over 50% of the methods require a loop invariant describing properties of arrays when using SPARK's VCGen approach. For example, LinkedSet.Get_Value requires a complex loop invariant that depends on logic encoded in the helper function contains—which would either need to be coded in logical form or axiomatized in the FDL proof language (either approach would be very difficult and would likely fall outside of the scope of effort that a typical developer would be expected to expend). Kiasan allows developers to obtain effective bounded contract checking without having to add these loop invariants.

**Verification Conditions:** A **VC** column entry of $X/Y$ indicates that $X$ VCs were automatically discharged by SPARK out of $Y$ generated VCs. Our experiments show that almost any contract that requires quantification (often required by functions that manipulates arrays) will have undischarged VCs. To give an indication of the amount of effort required to manually discharge VCs in the SPARK Proof Checker[4], a faculty member of our team with extensive experience in automated proof checking used the Proof Checker to prove the 3 undischarged VCs from one of our simplest examples—Value_Present which looks for an occurrence of a specified value in an array; 4 out of 7 of the VCs (those dealing with simple range checks on integer subtypes and array bounds) were automatically discharged by SPARK. Of the 3 remaining, 2 of the VCs required two proof steps to discharge while one required ten steps. Our best estimate is that it would take a Proof Checker *expert* user approximately 15 minutes to proof these three VCs. Given that the more realistic examples that we considered are much more complicated, we can conclude that it is extremely unlikely that the SPARK tool chain would be used in its present form by typical developers to check contracts other than those that capture simple numeric constraints (though it is possible that the Proof Checker could be used by verification engineers in an extensive verification period at the conclusion of development). In contrast, Kiasan provides effective bounded contract checking automatically for *all* the methods in all of our examples. Thus, it significantly improves the accessibility and usefulness of SPARK contracts.

Regarding **Question (II)**, as discussed in the previous section, checking must be bounded for Kiasan checking to be tractable. The bounding philosophy used here is similar to that of Alloy [20]—bounded verification with relatively small bounds can be very useful in uncovering program flaws (in design and implementation). Moreover, due to the bounded nature of SPARK, we believe our bounded approach fits well with how developers use SPARK. Table 1 shows timing data (in seconds) with array sizes from $k = 3 \dots 8$ elements (an exception is the MMR, which uses two-dimensional arrays of size 3 and a single dimensional array of size 9). The data shows that contract checking for even an entire package (except the MMR.Route) can be completed in 1-2 seconds for bounds of $k = 3, 4$ – indicating that Kiasan is clearly viable for incorporation in the code/test/debug loop of the developers. As an indication of how the performance scales, when we increased the array size for the **LinkedSet** example to 8, Delete and Get_Value completed in under 3 seconds each while Add required just over 6 minutes. This suggests that Kiasan could be deployed to check within small bounds during typical development activity, and then applied to check within larger bounds over night.

## 7. RELATED WORK

Our long term research plan seeks to demonstrate that SymExe can serve as a true verification technique (albeit bounded at this point) that can provide high confidence in the domain of embedded safety/security-critical systems in a highly automated fashion. As part of our effort to provide a rigorous foundation for SymExe, in previous work we have justified SymExe execution algorithms by providing proofs of correctness for complex optimizations [5, 11] and by providing mathematical approaches to calculate minimum number of test-cases and execution paths needed to achieve exhaustive exploration of program's data state [12].

There has been a lot of work on SymExe for programs that manipulate dynamically-allocated structures (for example, [22, 17, 28, 16, 29, 6]). Bakar Kiasan directly leverages existing decision procedures on complex structures (i.e., records and arrays) when it is

[4]Proof Checker is SPARK's interactive prover.

in logical representation mode [24]. This is similar to symbolic execution approaches that use a logical approach such as XRT [17] (and many others), however, without the complication of modeling program heap and pointer aliasing due to SPARK characteristics. When graph-based symbolic representation is used, the underlying algorithm in Bakar Kiasan is an adaptation of lazy initialization algorithms that were designed for Java [11], but optimized for inherent properties of SPARK programs. In addition, we focus on bounded verification of program behavioral contracts, as opposed to mainly finding bugs.

Carrying out work that is crucial for moving the SPARK infrastructure forward, Jackson and Passmore [21] aim to improve the usability of SPARK by building the Victor [30] tool that translates SPARK VCs to the various SMT solvers including Z3 [10], CVC3 [3], and Yices [13]. They note that concerns over the cost of handling non-automatically proven VCs cause "most SPARK users [to] settle for verifying little more than the absence of run-time exceptions caused by arithmetic overflow, divide by zero, or array bounds violations" and that "the number of non-automatically-proved VCs is usually significant." Using examples that primarily consist of VCs from run-time checks instead of full contracts, they show that using SMT solvers instead of the SPARK tooling discharges roughly the same number of VCs, but provides better performance and better error explanations. Their conclusions substantiate our arguments that, even though better support for VC proving can improve the SPARK tools, substantially increasing the automation of VC proving is difficult even with state-of-the-art solvers. In our opinion, this provides addition justification for considering a tool like Bakar Kiasan to complement VC proving by trading off complete verification for highly-automated bounded checking of expressive contracts.

Other closely related tool and verification technology efforts for SPARK and Ada include the AdaCore Hi-Lite Project and CodePeer Tool Set jointly maintained by AdaCore and SofCheck. Hi-Lite [19] aims to provide contract checking for a larger subset of Ada than SPARK and uses contract notations to be included in Ada 2012. Our work shares with Hi-Lite the goal of integrating unit testing and unit proof in SPARK/Ada (Hi-Lite also addresses C through the Frama C tool chain [15]). The primary differences lie in the verification technology. While both Bakar Kiasan and Hi-Lite seek to leverage SMT solvers to automate program reasoning, our symbolic execution approach is based on interpretive forward reasoning (in essence, strongest postcondition construction), while Hi-Lite adopts a backwards reasoning approach (in essence, weakest precondition construction) based on verification condition generation which separates logical constraint generation and constraint solving into two distinct phases. The practical impact of these technical differences is that our approach is generally more automated and can handle more complex data structures with greater automation and without the need for loop invariants to be supplied. In addition, the interpretive nature of symbolic execution allows very user-friendly presentations of state visualizations, contract violation counter examples, and summary of logical constraints along program execution paths – all of which we have illustrated in this paper. The greater automation in Bakar Kiasan is achieved by adopting a *bounded* checking approach – in essence, we trade off full verification to obtain a higher degree of automation. In contrast, the VCGen approach of Hi-Lite, though highly automated for reasoning about scalar data, requires loop invariants and manual interactions with lower-level theorem proving tools when handling complex data structures like the ones presented in this paper. However, in contrast with our work, the Hi-Lite tool chain does provide a path to full verification by factoring through the Why [14] intermediate language and ultimately translating to the Coq proof assistant [9]. With regard to unit testing, our approach currently offers a much more automated approach to test case generation, especially in the case of complex data structures. In summary, our symbolic execution approach appears to be complementary to the VCGen approach used in Hi-Lite, and one can certainly imagine a very synergistic integration of the two technologies where Bakar Kiasan is used earlier in life cycle with Hi-Lite technology following later. Indeed, we have had discussions with AdaCore engineers about possible integration of Bakar Kiasan with Hi-Lite. It would be interesting to work with the Hi-Lite team to explore how Hi-Lite tools might handle the examples that we have presented.

CodePeer [8] provides a variety forms of static analysis for full Ada including some similar in spirit to SPARK's Examiner analysis. CodePeer also provides a limited form of automated contract inference – limited in the sense that it primarily performs well on constraints on scalar data and could not automatically infer that types of contracts that we have illustrated in this paper. Thus, CodePeer is a bit less related to our goals compared to Hi-Lite, and one could also imagine symbolic execution techniques working in a complementary fashion with CodePeer. In our previous work, we have demonstrated how symbolic execution techniques can provide effective unit checking of procedure contracts for programs with complex manipulation of heap data [11], so there is good evidence to suggest that our approach can scale beyond SPARK to a larger subset of Ada that includes heap-allocated objects.

# 8. CONCLUSION AND FUTURE WORK

We have illustrated how symbolic execution techniques can increase the practicality of contract-based specification and checking in development of safety and security critical embedded systems. These techniques are complementary and can be used in conjunction with other contract verification techniques such as VCGen that more directly target full functional verification. SymExe hits a "sweet spot" between trade-offs of: the completeness of full functional verification to obtain a much greater degree of automation, the ability to more naturally blend processing of declarative and executable specifications, better support for error trace explanation and visualization, and stronger connections to other quality assurance methods such as testing. Although we have illustrated these techniques in the context of SPARK, they can be adapted easily to other contexts as well, *e.g.*, for safety critical subsets of C with contract languages [15]. In the case of the current SPARK tool chain, SymExe can play a key role in moving the SPARK contract framework from a method that is rarely used into one that is quite usable and quite effective in development of critical systems.

Our experience in using the SPARK contract language has exposed the need for several extensions including first class support for specifying package and invariants and data refinement. We are also investigating how our previous work on contract extensions supporting rich secure information flow specifications [1] can be integrated with the work presented here.


# Acknowledgements

The authors would like to thank Rod Chapman (Altran Praxis), Wes Embry and Yannick Moy (AdaCore), and Matt Wilding and David Greve (Rockwell Collins) for comments and suggestions on earlier versions of this work.

## 9. REFERENCES


[1] T. Amtoft, J. Hatcliff, E. Rodríguez, Robby, J. Hoag, and D. Greve. Specification and checking of software contracts for conditional information flow. In *15th International Symposium on Formal Methods (FM)*, pages 229–245. Springer, 2008.

[2] J. Barnes. *High Integrity Software – the SPARK Approach to Safety and Security*. Addison-Wesley, 2003.

[3] C. Barrett and C. Tinelli. CVC3. In *19th International Conference on Computer Aided Verification (CAV)*, volume 4590 of *Lecture Notes in Computer Science*, pages 298–302. Springer, 2007.

[4] J. Belt, J. Hatcliff, Robby, P. Chalin, D. Hardin, and X. Deng. Bakar kiasan: Flexible contract checking for critical systems using symbolic execution. In *NASA Formal Methods*, volume 6617 of *Lecture Notes in Computer Science*, pages 58–72. Springer, 2011.

[5] J. Belt, Robby, and X. Deng. Sireum/Topi LDP: A lightweight semi-decision procedure for optimizing symbolic execution-based analyses. In *Proceedings of the ACM SIGSOFT Symposium on the Foundations of Software Engineering (ESEC/FSE)*, pages 355–364, 2009.

[6] C. Cadar, D. Dunbar, and D. R. Engler. Klee: Unassisted and automatic generation of high-coverage tests for complex systems programs. In *8th USENIX Symposium on Operating Systems Design and Implementation (OSDI)*, pages 209–224. USENIX Association, 2008.

[7] B.-Y. E. Chang and K. R. M. Leino. Inferring object invariants: Extended abstract. *Electr. Notes Theor. Comput. Sci.*, 131:63–74, 2005.

[8] AdaCore/SofCheck CodePeer tool set. `http://www.adacore.com/home/products/codepeer/toolset/`.

[9] The Coq proof assistant. `http://coq.inria.fr/`.

[10] L. M. de Moura and N. Bjørner. Z3: An efficient SMT solver. In *Tools and Algorithms for the Construction and Analysis of Systems (TACAS)*, volume 4963 of *Lecture Notes in Computer Science*, pages 337–340. Springer, 2008.

[11] X. Deng, J. Lee, and Robby. Efficient symbolic execution algorithms for programs manipulating dynamic heap objects. Technical Report SAnToS-TR2009-09-25, Kansas State University, September 2009.

[12] X. Deng, R. Walker, and Robby. Program behavioral benchmarks for evaluating path-sensitive bounded verification techniques. Technical Report SAnToS-TR2010-08-20, Kansas State University, 2010.

[13] B. Dutertre and L. de Moura. The Yices SMT solver. Tool paper at http://yices.csl.sri.com/tool-paper.pdf, August 2006.

[14] J. C. Filliâtre and C. Marché. The why/krakatoa/caduceus platform for deductive program verification. In *Proceedings of the 19th international conference on Computer aided verification*, CAV'07, pages 173–177, Berlin, Heidelberg, 2007. Springer-Verlag.

[15] Frama-C website. `http://frama-c.com/`.

[16] P. Godefroid, N. Klarlund, and K. Sen. DART: Directed automated random testing. In *ACM SIGPLAN 2005 Conference on Programming Language Design and Implementation (PLDI)*, pages 213–223. ACM Press, 2005.

[17] W. Grieskamp, N. Tillmann, and W. Schulte. XRT–exploring runtime for .NET: Architecture and applications. *Workshop on Software Model Checking*, 2005.

[18] S. L. Hantler and J. C. King. An introduction to proving the correctness of programs. *ACM Computing Surveys (CSUR)*, 8(3):331–353, September 1976.

[19] The AdaCore Hi-Lite project. `http://www.open-do.org/projects/hi-lite/`.

[20] D. Jackson. Alloy: a lightweight object modelling notation. *ACM Transactions on Software Engineering and Methodology (TOSEM)*, 11(2):256 – 290, apr 2002.

[21] P. Jackson and G. Passmore. Proving SPARK verification conditions with SMT solvers, 2009. Draft journal article. `http://homepages.inf.ed.ac.uk/pbj/papers/vct-dec09-draft.pdf`.

[22] S. Khurshid, C. S. Păsăreanu, and W. Visser. Generalized symbolic execution for model checking and testing. *Tools and Algorithms for Construction and Analysis of Systems (TACAS)*, pages 553–568, 2003.

[23] J. C. King. Symbolic execution and program testing. *Communications of the ACM*, 19(7):385–394, 1976.

[24] D. Kroening and O. Strichman. *Decision Procedures – An Algorithmic Point of View*. Springer, 2008.

[25] K. R. M. Leino and F. Logozzo. Loop invariants on demand. In K. Yi, editor, *APLAS*, volume 3780 of *Lecture Notes in Computer Science*, pages 119–134. Springer, 2005.

[26] B. Rossebo, P. Oman, J. Alves-Foss, R. Blue, and P. Jaszkowiak. Using SPARK-Ada to model and verify a MILS message router. In *Proceedings of the International Symposium on Secure Software Engineering*, 2006.

[27] J. Rushby. The design and verification of secure systems. In *8th ACM Symposium on Operating Systems Principles*, volume 15(5), pages 12–21, 1981.

[28] K. Sen and G. Agha. CUTE: A concolic unit testing engine for C. In *ACM SIGSOFT Symposium on the Foundations of Software Engineering (FSE)*, pages 263–272, 2005.

[29] N. Tillmann and J. de Halleux. Pex–white box test generation for .NET. In *2nd International Conference on Tests and Proofs (TAP)*, volume 4966 of *Lecture Notes in Computer Science*, pages 134–153. Springer, 2008.

[30] Victor website. `http://homepages.inf.ed.ac.uk/pbj/spark/victor.html`.

# An Ada Design Pattern Recognition Tool for AADL Performance Analysis

Vincent Gaudel
Frank Singhoff
Alain Plantec
Stéphane Rubini
LISyC/EA 3883, University of Brest
20, av Le Gorgeu
CS 93837, 29238 Brest Cedex 3, France
{gaudel,singhoff,plantec,rubini}@univ-brest.fr

Pierre Dissaux
Jérôme Legrand
Ellidiss Technologies
24, quai de la douane
29200 Brest, France
{pierre.dissaux,jerome.legrand}@ellidiss.com

## ABSTRACT

This article deals with performance verification of architecture models of real-time embedded systems. Although real-time scheduling theory provides numerous analytical methods called feasibility tests for scheduling analysis, their use is a complicated task. In order to assist an architecture model designer in early verification, we provide an approach, based on real-time specific design patterns, enabling an automatic schedulability analysis. This analysis is based on existing feasibility tests, whose selection is deduced from the compliance of the system to a design pattern and other system's properties. Those conformity verifications are integrated into a schedulability tool called Cheddar. We show how to model the relationships between design patterns and feasibility tests and design patterns themselves. Based on these models, we apply a model-based engineering process to generate, in Ada, a feasibility test selection tool. The tool is able to detect from an architecture model which are the feasibility tests that the designer can apply. We explain a method for a designer willing to use this approach. We also describe the design patterns defined and the selection algorithm.

## Categories and Subject Descriptors

SOFTWARE ENGINEERING [**Software/Program Verification**]: Validation

## General Terms

Performance, Reliability, Verification.

## Keywords

AADL, Cheddar, Ada framework, Design Patterns, Real-time schedulability analysis, Platypus



## 1. INTRODUCTION

A real-time system is called critical when its dysfunction could lead to serious damages upon persons or the environment. The validation of such systems is therefore crucial. Real-time scheduling theory provides tools to validate such systems, especially analytical methods called *feasibility tests*. Yet, their use implies a high level of expertise in the real-time scheduling theory: the common draw to all these feasibility tests is that they need the system to fulfill a set of specific assumptions called *applicability constraints*. Those are based on architectural and environmental properties. Unfortunately, the large number of feasibility tests and applicability constraints complicates the use of such methods. That may explain why they are unused in many practical cases, although it could be profitable.

In our approach, we aim to help real-time architecture designers by automatically select relevant feasibility tests. To do so, we explicitly model relationships between architectural models and real-time scheduling analysis. The modeling of relationships is provided by a set of real-time design patterns for whom we are able to select applicable feasibility tests [5, 13].

We have provided five design patterns based on AADL (*Architecture Analysis and Description Language* [15]) communication and synchronization protocols between tasks. We model those design patterns by sets of assumptions on properties of architectural models. We analyze architectural models to verify their compliance to design patterns. When an architecture is compliant with one design pattern, we automatically propose to the designer to compute a set feasibility tests assigned to the corresponding design pattern.

In this article, we present a prototype which is able to select feasibility tests applicable to an architecture model compliant to a design pattern. This prototype is integrated with the performance analysis environment Cheddar and is generated by a model driven engineering process. We present our approach from a designer's perspective. We show how to model relationships between architectural properties and a set of feasibility tests. Then, we present an algorithm to analyze compliance of an architecture model to a design pattern and finally, we explain how we can generate our Ada prototype from our feasibility tests and design pattern models.

This article is organized as follows. In section 2 we present the approach from the designer's point of view. Section 3 contains a description of our five design patterns. Section 4 presents the architecture model of a simplified automotive system as a case study. Then, in section 5 the algorithm is presented. In section 6 we explain our engineering process and present the prototype evaluation. Related works follow in section 7, before conclusion in section 8.

## 2. PROPOSED APPROACH

In this section, we describe what we call feasibility tests and applicability constraints. Then we give a brief presentation of our five design patterns, followed by the description of the proposed method from the designer's perspective.

### 2.1 The issue of critical system schedulability analysis

Real-time scheduling theory enables designers to analyze the temporal behavior of a set of tasks with the use of analytical methods called feasibility tests. For example, Liu and Layland [10] have defined periodic tasks characterized by three parameters: deadline ($D_i$), period ($P_i$), and capacity ($C_i$). Each time a task $i$ is activated, it has to perform a job whose execution time is bounded by $C_i$ units of time before $D_i$ units of time after the task release time. Those parameters are used to compute some feasibility tests. Feasibility tests evaluate different performance criteria: processor utilization factor, worst case response time, deadlocks and priority inversions due to data access, memory footprint analysis, etc. Liu *et al.* have proposed equation (1) to perform schedulability analysis. This feasibility test computes the processor utilization factor for a system compliant with the following assumptions: all tasks must be periodic, independent and synchronous [7]; the scheduling protocol must be preemptive *Earliest Deadline First* or preemptive *Least Laxity First*.

$$U = \sum_{i=1}^{n} \frac{C_i}{P_i} \leq 1 \qquad (1)$$

This feasibility test is a necessary and a sufficient condition if $\forall i : \mathrm{D}_i = \mathrm{P}_i$.

We see that applying a feasibility test to a system implies that the system has to meet a set of architectural assumptions. In the next sections, those assumptions will be called *"applicability constraints"*. An applicability constraint expresses properties of architecture components such as task periodicity, scheduling protocol, communication protocol, etc.

### 2.2 Design pattern description

In order to select applicable feasibility tests, we have defined five real-time design patterns: *Synchronous data-flow*, *Ravenscar*, *Blackboard*, *Queued buffer* and *Unplugged*. Each of those design patterns provides an architectural solution to a synchronization problem between tasks by defining an inter-task communication protocol. There exists numerous other synchronization paradigms that could justify such specification. We use a pragmatic approach: the previous design patterns are all related to standards or industrial practices. For example, *Synchronous data-flow* implements Meta-H communication paradigms [20]. *Ravenscar* is related to the Ada 2005 Ravenscar profile [2]. *Blackboard* and *Queued buffer* model communication services that exist in ARINC 653 [1].

We assume that architecture models potentially compliant with our design patterns are written in AADL (*Architecture Analysis and Description Language* [15]). AADL is a textual and graphical architecture design language for model-based engineering of real-time systems.

The five design patterns work as follows:

1. **Synchronous data-flow** achieves data sharing through AADL data ports. Each task reads its input data ports at dispatch time and writes its output data ports at completion time. The execution platform deals with the data synchronization: there is no explicit protocol needed.

2. In **Ravenscar**, data are shared asynchronously, under the control of inheritance ceiling priority protocol. Ravenscar allows tasks to share data protected by semaphores. Semaphores can be used to build multiple synchronization protocols such as critical sections, readers/writers, producers/consumers, etc.

3. **Blackboard** implements the readers/writers communication protocol: only the last value produced can be consumed by tasks.

4. **Queued buffer** implements the producers/consumers communication protocol: messages are handled by a FIFO protocol.

5. **Unplugged** models independent tasks: tasks that do not communicate with each other.

### 2.3 Method from designer perspective

In the previous section, we have described feasibility tests and real-time design patterns. In this one, we define how we intend to assist real-time architecture designers. Figure 1 describes the method for designing an architecture model with the use of our design patterns. (1) A designer provides an architecture model. (2) An analysis is performed upon the architecture model in order to check its compliance to one of our design patterns. (4) Once the compliance to a design pattern is met, we provide a list of feasibility tests, (6) and we compute them to perform schedulability analysis.

During each of steps 2, 4 and 6, the designer may have to come back to the design phase. First at step (3), when we check the compliance of the architecture model to a design pattern: if it is not compliant, we are not able to provide a list of feasibility tests, so we give to the designer information (metrics and non-met applicability constraints) in order to assist him to fulfill the compliance of his architecture model to a real-time design pattern. During step (4), if the list of feasibility tests does not satisfy the designer (he might want to use a particular feasibility test or the list of selected feasibility tests may not be sufficient to prove the schedulability of the system), we provide alternative lists of feasibility tests and the reasons for their non-selection (5). Finally, once the schedulability analysis has proceeded, the designer may have to loop if the model is not schedulable (7).

## 3. HOW WE MODEL DESIGN PATTERNS

In order to perform the analysis explained in the previous section, we model different entities implied in the feasibility

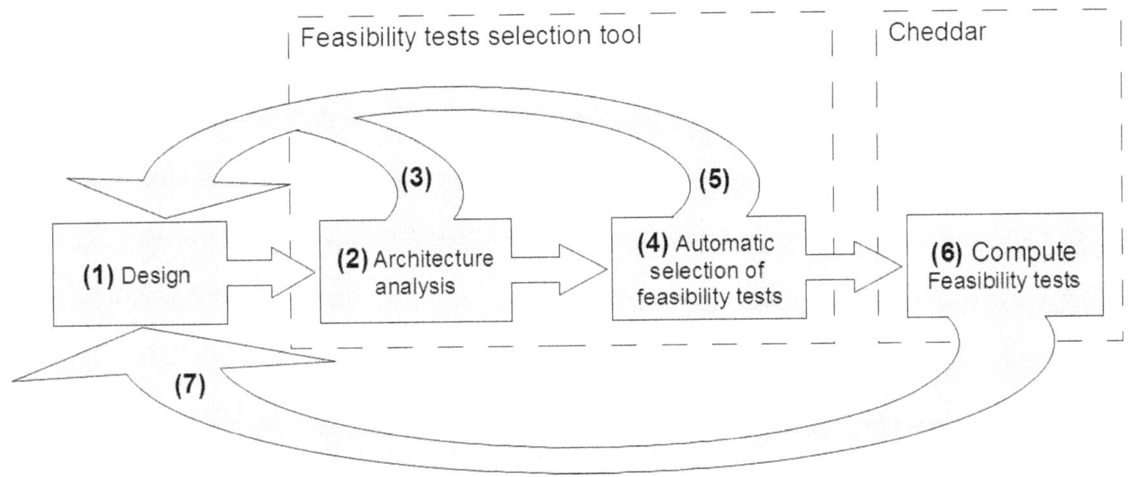


Figure 1: Method from the designer's perspective.

tests selection. In this section, we first present the language we use to model our design patterns. Then we describe how we model the relationships between architectural models and feasibility tests.

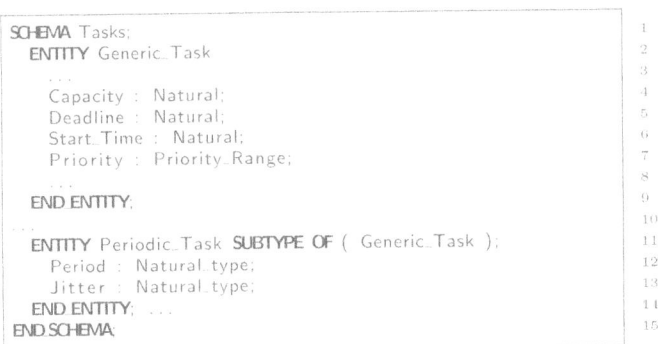

```
SCHEMA Tasks;
  ENTITY Generic_Task
    ...
    Capacity : Natural;
    Deadline : Natural;
    Start_Time : Natural;
    Priority : Priority_Range;
    ...
  END_ENTITY;
...
  ENTITY Periodic_Task SUBTYPE OF ( Generic_Task );
    Period : Natural_type;
    Jitter : Natural_type;
  END_ENTITY; ...
END_SCHEMA;
```

Figure 2: Excerpt from Cheddar meta-model: Generic_Task and Periodic_Task entities.

Our approach is developed within the Cheddar Project [18], an analysis environment for real-time applications written in Ada. Cheddar already implements numerous feasibility tests. Yet, an architecture designer has to select feasibility tests applicable to his architecture model, which is a hard task.

Cheddar provides an architecture language to model real-time systems. The architecture language is based on a meta-model. An instance within this meta-model is composed of several sets of entities: tasks, resources, dependencies, processors, buffers, networks and address spaces. The Cheddar meta-model is written in the EXPRESS language [19] and provides all the tools we need to model real-time design patterns. Figure 2 gives an excerpt of this meta-model. A generic task is defined by its capacity, its deadline, its release time and priority among others. A periodic task is defined as a generic task for which period and jitter are defined.

## 3.1 Structure of the EXPRESS models

In order to make explicit the relationships between architectural models and feasibility tests, we model design patterns by the applicability constraints they meet. Thus, de-

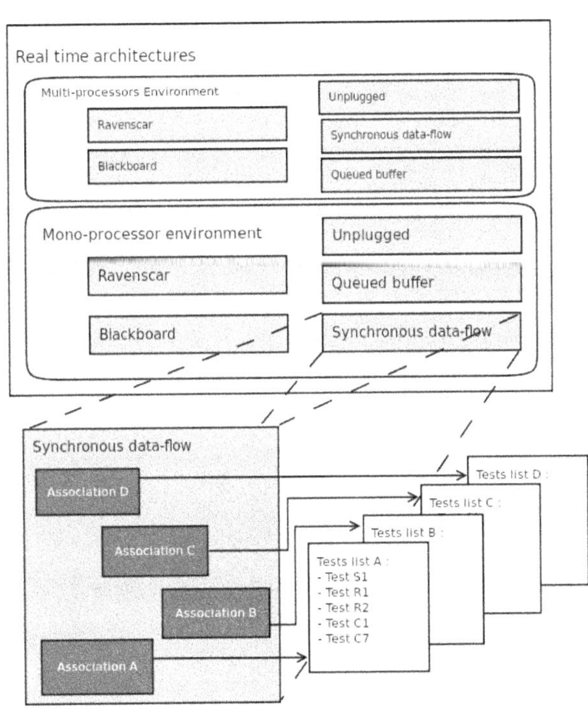


Figure 3: List of applicability constraints for feasibility tests selection.

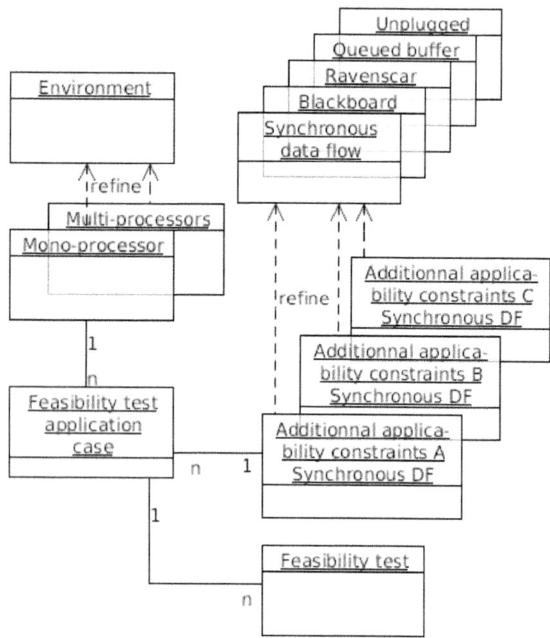


Figure 4: Association Model.

sign patterns are modeled, with EXPRESS, by sets of applicability constraints structured as follows.

Figure 3 represents the set of all real-time architecture types we can model with the Cheddar meta-model. Each box contains a subset of real-time architectures that meets the same applicability constraints. The more the background color of the boxes is dark, the more the number of met applicability constraints increases. There are various types of applicability constraints. Some are relative to the deployment environment: one cannot use the same feasibility tests for a mono-processor environment or a multi-processor environment (light gray). Others are relative to the used design pattern (medium gray). For each design pattern, we define several *associations* (dark gray) between additional applicability constraints and feasibility tests (126 for Synchronous data-flow). Applicability constraints are structured by environments, design patterns and associations. Figure 4 shows the association between those entities and feasibility tests.

## 3.2 How we model applicability constraints

For each subset of real-time systems (see. 3.1), we model all the applicability constraints with EXPRESS. For example, Synchronous data-flow applicability constraints on an architecture model are: (1) all tasks are periodic, (2) there is no buffer, (3) there is no data component, (4) data sharing protocol is sampled, immediate or delayed[1] and (5) there is no hierarchical scheduler (which means no shared address space between processors). EXPRESS enables the definition of *OCL(Object Constraint Language)-like* constraints [21] on the meta-model instances. Figure 5 gives the example of Synchronous data-flow applicability constraint number (1). This constraint is checked for all generic_task instances. It returns true when the size of the set of non-periodic tasks of the architecture model is equal to zero. The Cheddar

[1]Sampled, immediate and delayed are AADL communication protocols [15].

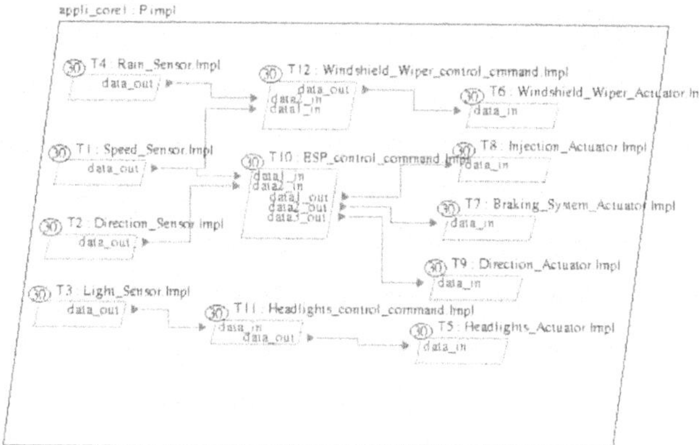


Figure 6: AADL graphic representation of the automotive architecture model.

meta-model is enriched by an *OCL-like* constraint for each applicability constraint.

# 4. CASE STUDY: EXAMPLE OF AN ARCHITECTURE MODEL COMPLIANT WITH SYNCHRONOUS DATA-FLOW

In this section, we present a case study of an architecture model compliant with Synchronous data-flow that will be used to illustrate the feasibility tests selection algorithm.

Let's consider a simplified version of an automotive embedded system. The architecture model is written in AADL. Figure 6 gives an AADL graphic representation of its architecture model. This system implements three functions: headlights control, windshield wiper control and ESC (Electronic Stability Control) which is a trajectory correction system. It contains twelve tasks communicating with each other through AADL data-ports. Each task reads its input memory slots at dispatch time and writes its output memory slots at completion time. There are four tasks reading sensor values (rain, speed, direction and light sensors) and five tasks sending instructions to actuators (windshield wiper, injection, braking system, direction and headlights actuators). The windshield wiper control task receives data from rain and speed sensors reading tasks and transmits a value to the task communicating with the windshield wiper actuator. The headlights control task receives data from light sensor reading task and transmits a value to the task communicating with the headlights actuator. The ESC control task receives data from speed and direction sensors reading tasks and transmits values to tasks communicating with injection, braking system and direction actuators.

All tasks have a 30ms period, a 30ms deadline and a 2ms capacity. The system is deployed on a mono-processor environment. All tasks are simultaneously released and the scheduling protocol is preemptive deadline monotonic. All five applicability constraints relative to the Synchronous data-flow design pattern are met: no buffer, nor data component, data sharing protocol is sampled and there are no shared address space between processors.

```
RULE all_tasks_are_periodic FOR ( generic_task );
WHERE
  R1 : SIZEOF ( QUERY ( t <* generic_task | NOT ( 'TASKS.PERIODIC_TASK' IN TYPEOF ( t ) ) ) ) = 0;
END_RULE;
```

Figure 5: Example of applicability constraint modeled in EXPRESS: Synchronous data-flow applicability constraint number (1).

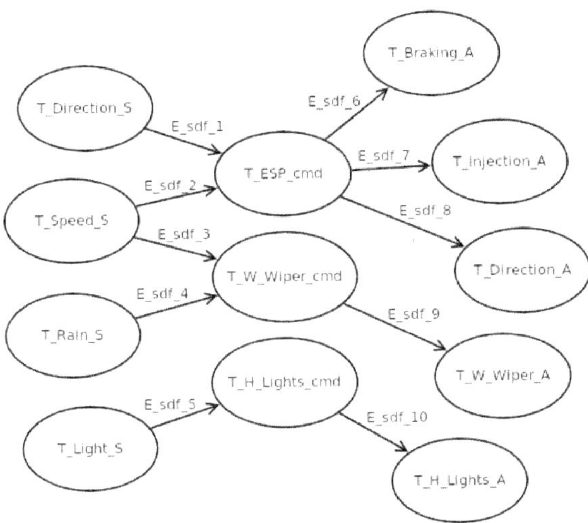


Figure 7: Graphic representation of dependency graph built in step 1.

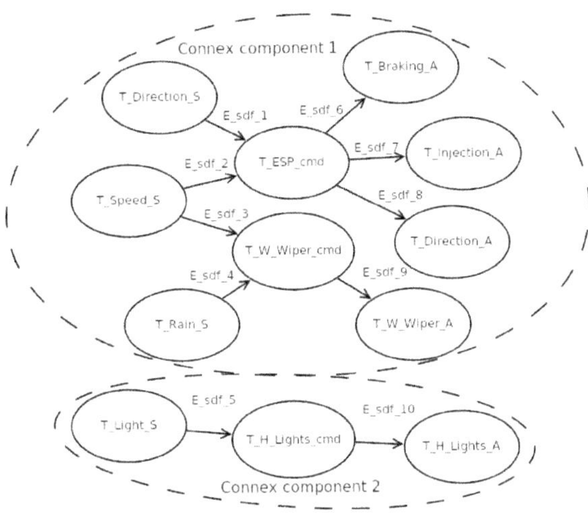


Figure 8: Connectivity components for synchronous data-flow edge in dependency graph built in step 1.

# 5. FEASIBILITY TESTS SELECTION ALGORITHM

In order to evaluate our approach, we implemented in Ada a prototype integrated into Cheddar. This section describes the algorithm used for the prototype. As we explained in section 2.3, the prototype analyses the compliance of an AADL architecture model to a design pattern, informs the designer of potential modifications of his architecture model and selects a list of feasibility tests. This algorithm is composed of four steps. In this section, we will describe it step by step and apply the steps to the case study presented in the previous section.

## 5.1 Step 1 : Model analysis to build Graph

The AADL architecture model is parsed by Cheddar, and stored as a set of Cheddar meta-model entities. Cheddar also computes dependencies between tasks for each data port communication, precedence constraint, shared data, message queue, etc.

An architecture model instance can be composed of several design patterns. Thus we have to identify which part of the system is a design pattern instance and the number and types of each design pattern instances. To do so, the first step builds a directed graph containing all tasks of the system and dependencies between those tasks. Thus, we create one node per task and one edge per dependency. Each dependency models a task synchronization or communication. There is one type of node and one type of edge for each dependency type (and then for each type of synchronization/communication).

Figure 7 gives the graphical representation of the dependency graph resulting of step 1 for the example of section 4. It contains twelve nodes and ten Synchronous data-flow edges.

## 5.2 Step 2 : Graph analysis to extract potential instances

Once the dependency graph is built, we look for subgraphs which are design pattern instances. Extracted subgraphs are called *potential instances*. We extract connectivity components for each type of edge. A connectivity component for one type of edge with no intersection with any other connectivity component is considered as a design pattern potential instance. If there is no potential instances, nodes and edges shared between two connectivity components are identified. Tasks and dependencies corresponding to those nodes and edges are the ones the designer has to modify in order to make his architecture model compliant with a design pattern.

Figure 8 represents the two connectivity components of the case study. The first one contains the three nodes relative to the headlights control tasks, and the second one the rest of the graph. Thus, there are two potential synchronous data-flow instances in the example.

## 5.3 Step 3 : Instantiation Confirmation

Each design pattern has a set of constraints. Extracted potential instances need to be analyzed in order to confirm actual design patterns instances. To do so, all potential instances are checked one by one by a verification of the applicability constraints relative to the design pattern.

For the simplified car system case study, all five applicability constraints of synchronous data-flow (see section 3.2) are

```
...
SCHEMA ASSOCIATION_17;
  USE FROM Mono_Processor_Environment;
  USE FROM Synchronous_Data_Flow;
  USE FROM Simultaneous_Release_Time_Constraint;
  USE FROM Period_Equal_Deadline_Constraint;
  USE FROM Preemptive_Deadline_Monotonic ;
  USE FROM Feasibility_tests_Taxonomy ( test_S1, test_C5,
      test_C7, test_R1, test_R2 );

END_SCHEMA;
....
```

**Figure 9: EXPRESS model of an association between feasibility tests, execution environment, design pattern and applicability constraints.**

checked for the two potential instances. Synchronous data-flow applicability constraints are met in our automotive system example. Then, two Synchronous data-flow instances are identified in this example.

## 5.4 Step 4 : Applicability constraints verification for feasibility tests selection

At the previous steps, we have verified that our architecture model is compliant with a design pattern. Now, we must find the feasibility tests that the designer is allowed to apply.

An association between a design pattern, its applicability constraints, an execution environment and a list of feasibility tests is modeled by an EXPRESS entity. Figure 9 gives an example of this type of entity for our automotive case study. Each **USE FROM** EXPRESS statement models one or several applicability constraints. If all **USE FROM** statements are met, it means that the feasibility tests listed in the EXPRESS entity can be applied on the architecture model.

In our automotive case study, five feasibility tests have been selected: one based on exhaustive simulation (test_S1), two based on processor utilization factor (test_C5, test_C7) and two based on worst case response time (test_R1, test_R2)[16].

# 6. PROTOTYPING AND EVALUATION

## 6.1 The prototype engineering protocol

One goal of our approach is to enable the creation of new design patterns at a meta-level. Thus, one can model a new design pattern and automate additional real-time scheduling theory knowledge. Figure 11 presents the prototype engineering/evaluation protocol. Based on the design patterns modeling, we first implemented manually a prototype integrated to Cheddar. This manually written version has been used to validate the design patterns modeling and the feasibility test selection algorithm. Once the prototype is evaluated, the Cheddar meta-model is enriched and checked within Platypus [14]. The Ada code of a new version of the prototype is then generated [12, 17]. For example, the Ada code generated for the applicability constraint presented in figure 5 is shown in figure 10.

At the time of the writing of this article, the prototype was able to recognize and select feasibility tests for the three design patterns: Synchronous Data Flow, Ravenscar and Unplugged, in the case of a mono-processor environment.

```
package body All_Tasks_Are_Periodic is

  function R1_QUERY1_Condition (t : Generic_Task_Ptr) return
        boolean is
  begin
    return not (Element_In_List (To_Unbounded_String("TASKS.
          PERIODIC_TASK"), Type_Of(t)));
  end R1_QUERY1_Condition;

function R1 (Sys : System) return boolean is
begin
  Context := Sys;
  return (Get_Number_Of_Elements(Select_And_Copy (sys.Tasks,
        R1_QUERY1_Condition'Access)) = Generic_Task_Set.
        Element_Range(0));
end R1;

end All_Tasks_Are_Periodic;
```

**Figure 10: Generated Ada package for a given applicability constraint: "All task are periodic".**

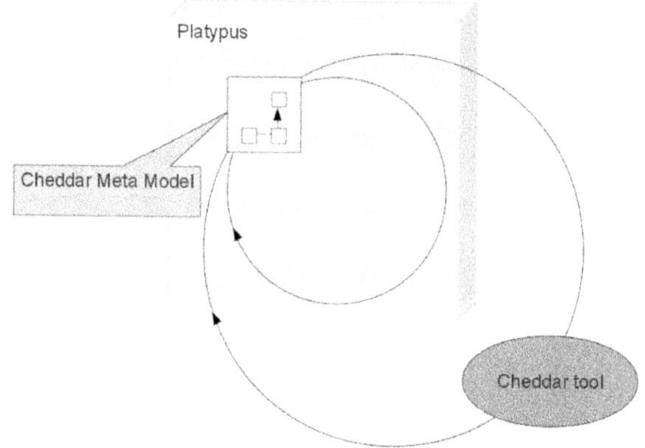


**Figure 11: Prototype engineering protocol.**

## 6.2 Evaluation

For the evaluation of our approach and the prototype, we aim to validate multiple points: the prototype itself (robustness, scaling, generated applicability constraints, ...) and the approach. Thus, the evaluation is divided in two parts. The first one consists in testing the implementation of the prototype with generated architectures covering all applicability constraints and design patterns. The second one consists in testing our approach with case studies.

### *6.2.1 Evaluation of generated architectures*

We have designed an architecture generator. Architectures generation is parameterizable. The parameters are the elements of generated architectures: for each generation, we choose which elements to generate and their numbers. The elements taken into account are the following: processor, core, task, buffer, dependency, message, resource and address space.

First, we generate architectures compliant with one design pattern, with a varying number of tasks and communication. Second, we generate architectures that are not compliant with any design patterns: an architecture model is generated for each applicability constraint. For example, a synchronous data flow instance with an extra sporadic task is generated in order to evaluate the constraint *all tasks are periodic*. At last set of architecture model is generated randomly. Figure 12 gives an overview of the number of generated architectures.

In the sequel, we selected feasibility tests for each generated architecture. The names of selected feasibility tests for each architecture, or the non-compliance to a design pattern, are stored in a file. Based on the AADL documentation, the selection or non-selection of feasibility tests for each architecture is then manually validated.

| Design Patterns | Number of Generated architectures |
|---|---|
| Synchronous_data_flow | 40 |
| Ravenscar | 40 |
| Unplugged | 40 |
| Uncompliant | 16 |
| Random | 40 |

**Figure 12: Number of generated architectures compliant, or not, with a given design pattern.**

Figure 13 gives the response time of the design pattern recognition algorithm, depending on the number of tasks and dependencies. This evaluation has been performed under Ubuntu 10.04 on a processor Intel(R) Dual CPU T2330 1.60GHz with 2,0GiB RAM memory. This evaluation shows that our prototype is robust to scaling, which is important from an industrial perspective. Moreover, the computation time required to check the compliance and to select feasibility tests is linear to the number of tasks in the system. For the second set of generated architectures, all the unmet applicability constraints have been found. As pointed by figure 13, the response time of the design pattern recognition algorithm for large systems (1000 tasks and 1000 dependencies) is reasonable for an interactive design tool.

### 6.2.2 *Evaluation of case studies*

We have investigated two case studies : the automotive system presented in section 4 and the mars pathfinder architecture [4]. The feasibility tests selected for the automotive system are described in section 5.4. Those five feasibility tests are enough to prove the schedulability of the system.

The mars pathfinder architecture is an instance of the Ravenscar design pattern. It contains seven tasks. Four of them share a data component. The access to the shared data is made by a mutex. The tasks's priorities are static and the scheduling protocol is Rate Monotonic. With the use of our approach, we select five feasibility tests : one based on exhaustive simulation (test_S1), two based on processor utilization factor (test_C3, test_C4) and two based on worst case response time (test_R1, test_R2)[16].

## 7. RELATED WORKS

Multiples approaches also investigate the domain of constraints checking within real-time systems.

Gilles *et al.* define a constraint language for AADL called REAL (Requirement Enforcement Analysis Language)[8]. REAL is developed by Telecom-Paris-Tech and ISAE and should be adopted as an AADL standard annex. REAL enables one to express different kinds of constraints directly on AADL architecture models. Authors have shown it could be used to express applicability constraints similar to those we aim to model. OCL (Object Constraint Language) enables to express the same constraints we use, but for UML models[21]. Another specification approach related to our design patterns can be found in the HOOD method and in the definition of HRT-HOOD whose goal is to comply with the Ada Ravenscar model [3]. Panunzio *et al.* define an engineering process based on the RCM meta-model (Ravenscar Computation Model)[11]. Performance verifications are proceeded by the MAST framework [9]. Like Cheddar, MAST implements several feasibility tests. Finally, PPOOA proposes an approach similar to our design patterns [6]. PPOOA is implemented as an UML extension and provides a set of predefined synchronization mechanisms. Moreover, the authors underline the importance of applying feasibility tests early in the design process and use Cheddar to do so. Each of those methods studies the validation of a set of real-time architectures with a static number of design patterns. In our approach, we would like to let the designer specify new design patterns and automatically generate the validation tool.

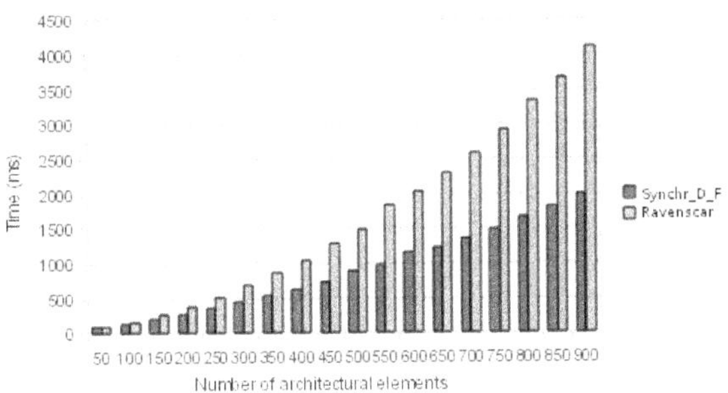


**Figure 13: Response times for the design pattern recognition algorithm in function of the number of tasks and dependencies (number of tasks = number of dependencies).**

## 8. CONCLUSION

In this article, we have presented an approach enabling the automatic selection of feasibility tests in order to do the verification of real-time systems. We have proposed a design method. We use design patterns based on inter-task communication protocols to reduce the diversity of architecture models. Thus, an algorithm was defined to check the compliance of the architecture model to a design pattern and to select a specific set of feasibility tests. In order to evaluate our work, we have generated code within Cheddar and made a prototype. Now, we will look for the analysis of more complex systems, resulting of design patterns composition. For now, we are able to compose design pattern two by two based on static rules. A second future work consists in designing a simple process to define new design patterns.

## 9. ACKNOWLEDGMENTS

We would like to thank Ellidiss Technologies and Region Bretagne for their support to this project.

## 10. REFERENCES


[1] Arinc. *Avionics Application Software Standard Interface*. The Arinc Committee, January 1997.

[2] A. Burns, B. Dobbing, and G. Romanski. The ravenscar tasking profile for high integrity real-time programs. In Lars Asplund, editor, *Reliable Software Technologies Ada-Europe*, volume 1411 of *Lecture Notes in Computer Science*, pages 263–275. Springer Netherlands, 1998.

[3] A. Burns and A.J. Wellings. *HRT-HOOD: a structured design method for hard real-time Ada systems*, volume 3. Elsevier Science, 1995.

[4] F. Cottet, J. Delacroix, C. Kaiser, and Z. Mammeri. *Scheduling in real-time systems*. Wiley Online Library, 2002.

[5] P. Dissaux and F. Singhoff. Stood and Cheddar : AADL as a Pivot Language for Analysing Performances of Real Time Architectures. Proceedings of the European Real Time System conference. Toulouse, France, January 2008.

[6] J. Fernández Sánchez and G. Mármol Acitores. Modelling and Evaluating Real-Time Software Architectures. *Reliable Software Technologies–Ada-Europe 2009, LNCS Springer, Volume 5570*, pages 164–176, 2009.

[7] L. George, N. Rivierre, and M. Spuri. Preemptive and Non-Preemptive Real-time Uni-processor Scheduling. INRIA Technical report number 2966, 1996.

[8] O. Gilles and J. Hugues. Expressing and enforcing user-defined constraints of AADL models. In *2010 15th IEEE International Conference on Engineering of Complex Computer Systems*, pages 337–342. IEEE, 2010.

[9] G. Harbour, G. Garcia, P. Gutierrez, D. Moyano, et al. MAST: Modeling and analysis suite for real time applications. In *Real-Time Systems, 13th Euromicro Conference on, 2001.*, pages 125–134. IEEE, 2002.

[10] C.L. Liu and J.W. Layland. Scheduling algorithms for multiprogramming in a hard-real-time environment. *Journal of the ACM (JACM)*, 20(1):46–61, 1973.

[11] M. Panunzio and T. Vardanega. A metamodel-driven process featuring advanced model-based timing analysis. In *Reliable software technologies: Ada-Europe 2007: 12th Ada-Europe International Conference on Reliable Software Technologies, Geneva, Switzerland, June 25-29, 2007: proceedings*, pages 128–141. LNCS Springer-Verlag New York Inc, Volume 4498, 2007.

[12] A. Plantec and F. Singhoff. Refactoring of an Ada 95 Library with a Meta CASE Tool. *ACM SIGAda Ada Letters, ACM Press, New York, USA*, 26(3):61–70, November 2006.

[13] A. Plantec, F. Singhoff, P. Dissaux, and J. Legrand. Enforcing applicability of real-time scheduling theory feasibility tests with the use of design-patterns. In Tiziana Margaria and Bernhard Steffen, editors, *Leveraging Applications of Formal Methods, Verification, and Validation*, volume 6415 of *Lecture Notes in Computer Science*, pages 4–17. Springer Berlin / Heidelberg, 2010.

[14] Platypus Technical Summary and download. http://cassoulet.univ-brest.fr/mme/, 2007.

[15] SAE. Architecture Analysis and Design Language (AADL) AS-5506A. Technical report, The Engineering Society For Advancing Mobility Land Sea Air and Space, Aerospace Information Report, Version 2.0, January 2009.

[16] F. Singhoff. A taxonomy of real-time scheduling theory feasibility tests. LISyC Technical report, number singhoff-01-2010, Available at http://beru.univ-brest.fr/~singhoff/cheddar, February 2010.

[17] F. Singhoff and A. Plantec. Towards User-Level extensibility of an Ada library : an experiment with Cheddar. Proceedings of the 12th International Conference on Reliable Software Technologies, Ada-Europe. LNCS Springer-Verlag, Volume 4498, pages 180-191, Geneva, June 2007.

[18] F. Singhoff, A. Plantec, P. Dissaux, and J. Legrand. Investigating the usability of real-time scheduling theory with the Cheddar project. *Real-Time Systems*, 43(3):259–295, 2009.

[19] P. Spiby. ISO 10303 industrial automation systems–product data representation and exchange–part 11: Description methods: The express language reference manual. *ISO DIS*, pages 10303–11, 1992.

[20] S. Vestal. Meta-H User's Manual, Version 1.27. Technical report, download at http://www.htc.honeywell.com/metah/uguide.pdf, 1998.

[21] Jos Warmer and Anneke Kleppe. *The Object Constraint Language: Getting Your Models Ready for MDA*. Addison-Wesley Longman Publishing Co., Inc., Boston, MA, USA, 2 edition, 2003.

# Improving Quality of Ada Software with Range Analysis

Jay Abraham
MathWorks
3 Apple Hill Drive
Natick, MA 01760, USA
1 (508) 647-3027
jabraham@mathworks.com

Jeff Chapple
MathWorks
3 Apple Hill Drive
Natick, MA 01760, USA
1 (508) 647-8045
jchapple@mathworks.com

Cyril Preve
MathWorks
100 C alle Saint-Exupery
Montbonnot 38330, France
33-4-56-80-6731
cpreve@mathworks.com

## ABSTRACT
Software in critical embedded systems used in aerospace, military, and transport applications, that is, systems where quality and reliability are imperative, continues to become more complex. For example, the Boeing 787 aircraft flight control system will have about 6.5 million lines of code [1], the avionics software for the F-22 Raptor consists of 1.7 million lines of code [2] and avionics software for the F-35 Joint Strike Fighter is expected to have 5.7 million lines of code [3]. The Ada programming language has been a key component in these applications and is a language of choice for critical systems where reliability matters. As these systems are becoming more sophisticated, software development organizations must meet stringent software quality objectives that are mandated by the organization itself or required by customers or by government regulations. For software teams to meet these objectives, and to ideally achieve software with minimal defects, the Ada programming language alone may not provide sufficient reliability margins. Coupling the Ada language with state of the art testing and verification solutions may improve the predictability of risk. This paper examines software verification and testing approaches that have been applied to Ada programs.

## Categories and Subject Descriptors
D.2.4 [**Software**]: Software / Program Verification – *correctness proofs, formal methods, reliability, validation.*

## General Terms
Reliability, Verification.

## Keywords
Static code analysis, abstract interpretation, code verification, variable range analysis, software quality assurance.



## 1. INTRODUCTION
Ada is a strong language with built-in mechanisms that naturally lead to less risky software programs. This is possible because Ada is a structured and strongly typed language with built-in run-time protection mechanisms. For example, subtyping allows for specification of ranges for variables. The compiler can detect illegal values for these variables as well as insert run-time range checks during compilation so that violating specified ranges result in a Constraint_Error during run-time.

In civil aerospace avionics that are governed by standards such as DO-178B, Ada is often used to implement critical electronic systems. The DO-178B standard specifies various forms of testing that must be performed on the software. These include requirements and coverage based testing. DO-178B stipulates that test-cases test for normal range and robustness testing to verify the software response to abnormal input values and initialization conditions, e.g. when a sensor fails and generateds spurious data on a bus [4].

This paper examines software verification and testing approaches that have been applied to Ada programs. These techniques have been applied to critical software projects in civil and military aerospace and defense projects over the past decade. Concrete technical examples will be explored to see how these verification techniques, in particular the use of range analysis can be used to improve the quality and reliability of complex software systems that are written in Ada.

## 2. Developing Software in Ada
Even though Ada is a strongly typed language, programmers may not take advantage of the protection offered by the language, thus resulting in errors that could occur during run-time. Additionally run-time errors that could result due to the misuse of the language or because of constraints imposed during software design and development. A few examples of run-time errors are provided below:

- Non-initialized data; if variables are not initialized, they will contain unknown values.
- Out of bounds array access, occurs when data is written or read beyond the boundary of allocated memory.
- Null pointer dereference, occurs when attempting to reference memory with a pointer that is null. Any dereference of that pointer will likely lead to a crash.

- Incorrect computation, caused by an arithmetic error such as an overflow, underflow, divide by zero, or when taking a square root of a negative number.
- Concurrent accesses to shared data, when two or more threads try to access the same memory location at the same time.
- Dead code, although dead code (i.e. code that will never execute) may not directly cause a run-time failure, it may be important to understand why the code will not execute.

The next section examines a few Ada code fragment examples identifying and explaining (via comments in the code) about how run-time errors could occur.

## 2.1 Division by Zero

```
procedure ZDVS(X : Integer) is
        I : Integer;
        J : Integer := 1;
begin
        I := 1024 / (J-X);          -- Scalar division
                                    -- by zero when
                                    -- procedure ZDVS is
                                    -- called with
                                    -- parameter 1
end ZDVS;

procedure ZDVF(Z : Float) is
        I : Float;
        J : Float := 1.0;
begin
        I := 1024.0 / (J-Z);        -- Possible float
                                    -- division by zero
end ZDVF;
```

## 2.2 Overflow of an Array Index

```
procedure OVFL_ARRAY is
        A : array(1..20) of Float;
        J : Integer;
begin
        for I in A'First .. A'Last loop
                A(I) := 0.0 ;
                J := I + 1;
        end loop;
        A(J) := 0.0; -- Overflow array
end OVFL_ARRAY;
```

## 2.3 Range Violation

```
type T is digits 4 range 0.0 .. 100.0;
subtype T1 is T
        digits 1000 range 0.0 .. 100.0;
        -- Digits value is too large,
        -- highest possible value is 4
```

# 3. When Quality and Reliability Matter

In situations where quality and reliability matter, it is imperative that the risk of run-time errors are minimized. However, practical considerations make it an arduous task to guarantee the elimination of run-time errors, because it is not practical to exhaustively test complex systems to prove that the software is run-time error free [5]. Here are examples of a few situations which can potentially introduce run-time errors in software written in the Ada programming language.

- Avionics applications that require I/O access to aircraft data buses typically access these buses via the low-level C style API libraries or assembler supplied with bus interface modules, for example a MIL-STD-1553. Since the interface to non Ada languages do not enjoy the benefits of run-time protection, it is possible that run-time errors could result as a consequence of the interface.
- There may be a need to bypass strong type checking by using unchecked conversion for example in the case of bus reading/writing or for performance reasons, resulting in non-protected software. Using subtypes (e.g. subtype S1 is T range 0..5;) will help to catch at compile time obvious errors such as X:=6. At run-time this will raise a Constraint_Error (X:=5; X:=X+1;), but there is run-time performance penalty as well as increase in size of the code. Therefore this run-time protection mechanism may only be used during testing phases but not in actual production and deployment.
- Using new types (example: type speed is 0..300 and type temp is 0..100 to make sure no operation will occur between variables of such type). This is often considered restrictive by developers and is often not used, increasing the risk for a run-time error.

# 4. Use of Ada in Critical Systems

Even though there is some risk of run-time errors when developing software programs using the Ada language, the use of this language for a variety of past and current projects is quite remarkable. This fact is due in part to Ada considered to be a robust language [6]. In fact, it is the only language to include a Safety and Security Annex as part of the LRM. A website maintained by Michael Feldman of the SIGAda Education Working Group catalogs the various projects that have used Ada. A few examples are shown in the lists below [7]:

- Air traffic management systems: Various countries in Asia, Europe, and the Americas
- Commercial aircraft: Airbus 320/330/340/380, Boeing 737-787, Saab 2000, Ilyushin 96M
- Railway transportation: French high speed rail (TGV), New York City subway, Swiss Federal Railways
- Commercial rockets: Ariane 4 and 5, Atlas V
- Satellites: Hughes 601/702, INMARSAT, Intelsat VII, NSTAR, Cassini, EOS, GOES, ...
- Millitary: USAF C-17/F-16/F-22, US Army M1A2/HAB, Eurocopter, EADS MRTT

The software in these applications must be maintained for the life of the equipment, often for tens of years. Maintenance involves updates to the software. Therefore, even if no new functionality is being developed, software teams must update legacy software. It is important to understand the run-time impact of such updates. For example, could changing a few lines of code in one Ada procedure impact another procedure? And how would these software teams exhaustively know that the changes they have made will not cause a run-time error in the modified procedure or some other downstream procedure?

# 5. Improving the Quality of Ada Software

Traditional means of testing software involves the use of manual code review and dynamic testing. Code review involves manual inspection of the source code [8]. The process involves a team that will perform the review (moderator, designer, coder, and tester), the preparation process (creation of a checklist), and the inspection itself. One of the objectives of the process is to find errors in code. The outcome may involve rework to address errors found and follow-up to ensure that issues and concerns raised during inspection are resolved. Detecting subtle run-time errors can be a difficult proposition. For example, an overflow or underflow due to complex mathematical operations that involve programmatic control could easily be missed during a code review.

Dynamic testing verifies the execution flow of software; e.g. decision paths, inputs and outputs. Dynamic testing involves the creation of test-cases and test-vectors and execution of the software against these tests. This particularly suits the goal of finding design errors, with test cases often matching functional requirements. Comparison of the results to expected or known correct behavior of the software is then performed.

Theoretically, exhaustively producing all test-cases and executing the right test case and observing the behavior of the software at the right time may identify all defects. But even simple programs with few inputs and outputs may require extremely large number of test-cases in order to produce exhaustive results. For complex systems, limiting the range of inputs will still produce a very large number of test-cases. Given schedule constraints, it is not be possible to perform exhaustive testing.

If it is possible to trace the ranges of variables in software, this method may provide some predictability to identify which parts of the software may or may not fail with a run-time error. Essentially this would verify the robustness of the software in an exhaustive manner. By utilizing this technique, one can take advantage of the benefits of the Ada language without necessarily having to write code in a specific manner. The advantage is that it one can then apply this retroactively to legacy code. It is also possible to understand the impact of modifying legacy code.

## 6. Formal Methods Techniques

In order to improve the robustness of Ada software, the verification process must provide guidance that run-time errors have been identified or that their absence can be demonstrated. Formal methods are techniques that can be utilized for this purpose. Formal methods use mathematical proofs as the basis of stating solutions to a problem. For example, demonstrating that a variable in software shall always have a positive value (i.e. it will not be negative). Coupled with static code analysis (i.e. analysis of software without dynamic execution), these techniques can propagate variable ranges in a model or code and identify certain run-time errors or prove their absence.

An example of a formal method based technique is abstract interpretation [9]. Explaining the operation of this technique is best accomplished by studying a simple example. Consider the multiplication of three large integers:

$$-4586 \times 34985 \times 2389 = ?$$

For the mathematical problem defined it is difficult to quickly compute the final value by hand. However, if we abstract the result of the computation to the sign domain (i.e., either positive, negative, or zero), it is easy to understand that the sign of the computation will be negative. Determining the sign for this mathematical computation is an application of abstract interpretation. The technique enables us to know precisely some properties of the final result, in this example, the sign, without having to multiply the integers fully. We also know that the sign will never be positive for this computation. In fact abstract interpretation will prove that the sign of the operation will always be negative and never positive or zero.

Let us now consider a simplified application of the formal mathematics of abstract interpretation to software programs. The semantics of a programming language is represented by the concrete domain $S$. Let $A$ represent the abstraction of the semantics. The abstraction function $\alpha$ maps from the concrete domain to the abstract domain. The concretization function $\gamma$ maps from the abstract domain $A$ to the concrete domain $S$. $\alpha$ and $\gamma$ form a Galois connection and are monotonic [10]. Certain proof properties of the software can be performed on the abstract domain $A$. It is a simpler problem to perform the proof on the abstract domain $A$ versus the concrete domain $S$.

The concept of soundness is important in context of a discussion on abstract interpretation. Soundness implies that when assertions are made about a property, those assertions are proven to be correct. The results from abstract interpretation are considered sound because it can be mathematically proven with structural induction that abstraction will predict the correct outcome. When applied to software programs, abstract interpretation can be used to prove certain properties of software, e.g., to prove that the software will not exhibit certain run-time errors [11].

## 7. Variable Range Analysis

Cousot and Cousot describe the application and success of abstract interpretation to static program analysis [12]. Deutsch describes the application of this technique to a commercial software tool [13]. The application of abstract interpretation involves computing approximate semantics of the software code with the abstraction function $\alpha$ such that it can be verified in the abstract domain. This produces equations or constraints whose solution is a computer representation of the program's abstract semantics.

Lattices are used to represent variable values. For the sign example described earlier, the lattice shown in Figure 1 can be used to propagate abstract values in a program (starting at the bottom and working to the top). Arriving at any given node in the lattice proves a certain property. Arriving at the top of the lattice indicates that a certain property is unproven.

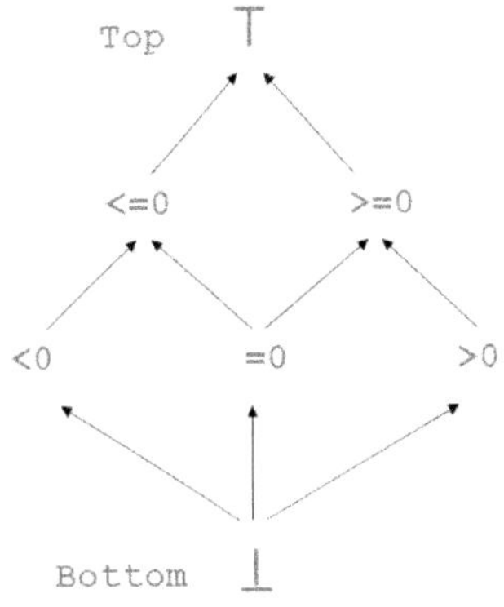


**Figure 1. Lattice representation of variables.**

Over approximation is applied to all possible execution paths in a program [10]. Techniques such as widening and narrowing and iteration with a solver are used to solve the equations and constraints to identify variable ranges and then use that information to prove the existence of or the absence of run-time errors in Ada source code.

To see the application of abstract interpretation to code verification, consider the following operation in Ada code:

X := X / (X – Y);

If X is equal to Y, then a divide by zero will occur. In order to conclusively determine if a divide by zero may or may not occur, the range of X and Y must be known. If the ranges overlap, than a divide by zero condition is possible.

Plotting X and Y as shown in Figure 2, one can see that the 45 degree line comprising of X=Y would result in a run-time error. The scatter plot shows all possible values of X and Y when the program executes this line of code (designated with +). Dynamic testing would utilize enumeration over various combinations of X and Y to determine if there will be a failure. However, given the large number of tests that would have to be run, this type of testing may not detect or prove the absence of the divide by zero run-time error.

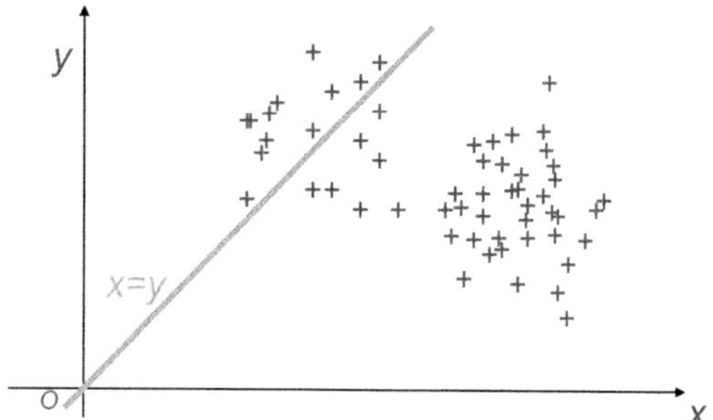


**Figure 2. Plot of data for X and Y.**

Another methodology would be to apply type analysis to examine the range of X and Y in context of the run-time error condition (i.e. X=Y). In Figure 3, note the bounding box created by type analysis. If the bounding box intersects X=Y, then there is a potential for failure. Some static code analysis tools apply this technique. However, type analysis in this case is too pessimistic, since it includes unrealistic values for X and Y.

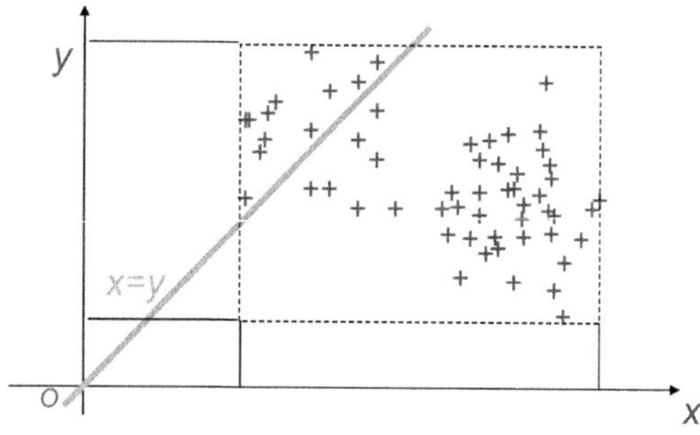


**Figure 3. Type analysis.**

With abstract interpretation, a more accurate representation of the data ranges of X and Y are created. Since various programming constructs could influence the values of X and Y (e.g., arithmetic operations, loops, if-then-else, multi-tasking, etc.) an abstract lattice is defined. A simplified representation of this concept is to consider the grouping of the data as polyhedron as shown in Figure 4. Since the polyhedron does not intersect X=Y we can conclusively say that a division by zero will not occur.

The abstract interpretation concept can be generalized as a tool set that can be used to determine variable ranges and to detect a wide range of run-time errors in software. Various types of tools that implement abstract interpretation can be found in academia and industry, with some tools supporting abstract interpretation based static code analysis of Ada software. A few broad examples of tools that implement abstract interpretation are provided below.

- Stacktool for stack overflow checking of software [14]
- DAEDALUS for validating critical software [15]
- JULIA for abstract interpretation verification of Java code [16]
- Polyspace for verification of Ada and C/C++ [17]

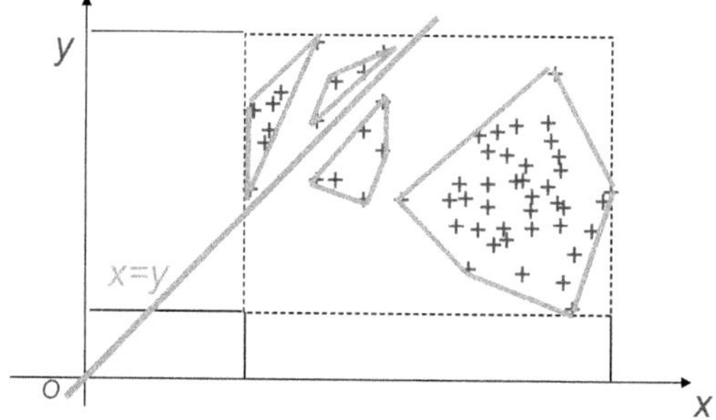


**Figure 4. Abstract interpretation.**

In this paper, we use Polyspace® as an example to explain how such a tool can help determine variable ranges and detect and prove the absence of run-time errors such as overflows and divide by zero conditions. The input to Polyspace is C, C++, or Ada source code. The output is source code painted in four colors.

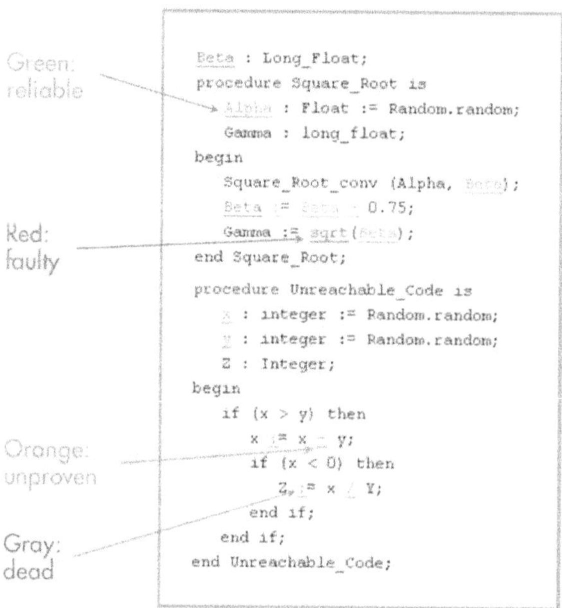


**Figure 5. Polyspace color-coding that indicates the status of each element in the code.**

As shown in Figure 5 Polyspace informs the user of the quality of the code using this four color coded scheme. Green indicates that the code is reliable and will not suffer from a run-time error. Red indicates a run-time error is certain to occur. Orange indicates that the tool was unable to prove if a run-time error will or will not occur, indicating that a run-time error may occur under some conditions. Gray indicates dead code or code that will not execute.

Using a tool tip mechanism, Polyspace also shows the ranges of variables directly on the source code. For example, as shown in Figure 6, Polyspace has determined that on line 121, the integer variable *cur* (highlighted with a circle) can only have the value of 2, 4, or range of 6..2147483644 (underlined). The variable *big* is a constant integer with the value 2^(30-3) which is 1073741821. The loop must iterate 2^31 times before *y > big* allows it to break from the loop. Without exhaustive testing, using Polyspace, one is able to determine that the operation *cur := cur + 2;* does not cause an overflow and that the loop is not infinite.

```
114     procedure Non_Infinite_Loop (X : out Integer) is
115        cur : Integer :=0;
116     begin
117        X := 0;
118        loop
119           exit when   >   ;
120           cur :=      2;
121           X :=        2;
122        end loop;
123        X :=      variable 'cur' (type: integer [-2^31 .. 2^31-1]): 2 or 4 or [6 .. 2147483644]
124     end Non_Infinite_Loop;
```

**Figure 6. Tool tip to show variable range information.**

## 8. Using Range Analysis to Improve Quality

This section explores various examples of Ada source code to highlight how one can use the range analysis information from Polyspace to understand how run-time errors could manifest. Ada source code fragments are shown with the color code results (with tool tips to show range information). An explanation is also provided.

```
147     Count := Populate_Integer(min=>5,max=>15);
148     if      > 10 then
149        for I in Two_Bit'First .. Two_Bit'Last loop
150           My_Status := Status Val(Two_Bit'Pos( ));
151        end loop;            variable 'I' (type: short_short_integer [0 .. 3]): full-range [0 .. 3]
152     end if;
153  exception

150           My_Status := Status Val(Two_Bit'Pos( ));
151        end loop;    assignment of variable 'My_Status' (type: status [0 .. 2]): full-range [0 .. 2]
152     end if;
```

**Figure 7. Polyspace results identifying Constraint_Error.**

In Figure 7, we can see that Polyspace found a run-time error (variable I colored in red) on line 149 and an unproven run-time check on line 150 (' colored in orange). Polyspace can see that there will be a Constraint_Error because the Two_Bit type through which the code iterates has a wider range than the Status type to which it is being converted. Note that the conversion is performed by taking the position of a value in the range of Two_Bit and finding the value of that position's enumeration in the Status type. Tool tips for I and ' on line 150 show the inconsistent ranges with the source range being wider than the target range. Hence the problem - and why the ' is orange. The diagnostic on line 149 shows the resultant problem (variable I colored in red).

```
94      if random > low_limit and then random < max and then           > 7.5 then
95         pi_squared :=    **2;
96         rhs_min := 2.0*      ;
97         rhs_mid := 3.0*      ;
98         rhs_max := 4.0*      ;
99         if     **2 - float(      )        then
100           c :=red;
101        end if;        variable 'random' (type: integer [-2^31 .. 2^31-1]): [2 .. 4]
```

**Figure 8. Polyspace results identifying unreachable code (line 100)**

In Figure 8, the assignment on line 100 is unreachable and has been colored in gray by Polyspace (:= is colored in gray in the figure above). The sequence can be followed with tool tips: random starts full range after the first comparison (> low_limit), it's range is 2..max_int. After comparison < max, it's range is 2..4 and (2..4)*two_pi cannot equal pi squared.

```
61      if Initialised then
62         if Count < Max then
63            Count := Count + 1;
64         end if;
65      else
66         Count := 0;
67         Sum := 1;
68         Initialised := True;
69      end if;
70      if Count > Max then
71         return;
72      end if;
73
74      if Initialised then
75        null;
76      end if;
77
78      Sum := Sum + 1;
79      Size := ...

78         Sum := Sum + 1;
79         Size :=
80         if        variable 'sum' (type: integer [-2^31 .. 2^31-1]): [1 .. 2^31-1]
```

**Figure 9. Polyspace results potential overflow condition (line 78)**

In Figure 9, Sum is only initialized sometimes. It depends on the path taken above line 78 and whether this procedure has been called before. The tool tip from Polyspace shows that Sum is full range and overflow is possible; we do not know how many times this procedure will be called. Therefore, there is a potential for an overflow when the add operation on line 78 occurs. Therefore the + is colored in orange.

## 9. Conclusion

The Ada programming language has been a key component in critical software and is a language of choice when quality and reliability matter. It is a strongly typed language with built-in run-time protection mechanisms that can lead to less risky software programs. In civil aerospace avionics that are governed by standards such as DO-178B, Ada is often used to implement critical electronic systems. As these systems are becoming more sophisticated, software development organizations must meet stringent software quality objectives that are mandated by the organization itself or required by customers or by government regulations. For software teams to meet these objectives, and to ideally achieve software with minimal defects, the Ada programming language alone may not provide sufficient reliability requirements margins.

Static code analysis coupled with formal methods to augment the capabilities of Ada may provide some assistance. In particular, using sophisticated tools with very accurate mechanisms to track variable ranges and use that information to identify where Ada software could fail or potentially fail. Information about variable ranges and places where run-time errors could occur provide guidance about the overall quality of the software. The process permits the identification of problems which can either be signed off as non issues or recorded as real problems that must be fixed.

## 10. ACKNOWLEDGMENTS

Our thanks to Patrick Munier and Christian Bard for their contribution in developing this paper.

## 11. REFERENCES

[1] Mecham, M. 2007. Boeing Faces Pretty Tight 787 Delivery Schedule. Aviation Week. 9 September 2007.

[2] Pace, S. 1999. F-22 Raptor: America's Next Lethal War Machine. Mcgraw-Hill.

[3] Goebel, G. 2001. The Lockheed Martin F-35 Joint Strike Fighter (JSF). http://www.vectorsite.net/avf35.html.

[4] Zemskyy D. Safety and Reliability Considerations in DO-178B.

[5] Pan, J. 1999. Dependable Embedded Systems. Software Testing.

[6] Reihle R. "Can Software Be Safe?-An Ada Viewpoint. Embedded Systems Programming.

[7] Feldman, M. Who is using Ada. http://www.seas.gwu.edu/~mfeldman/ada-project-summary.html.

[8] Fagan M. 1976. Design and Code Inspections to Reduce Errors in Program Development. IBM Systems Journal.

[9] Cousot, P. 1977. Abstract interpretation: a unified lattice model for static analysis of programs by construction or approximation of fixpoints. 4th ACM SIGACT-SIGPLAN symposium on Principles of programming languages.

[10] Cousot P., Cousot R. 1992. Comparing the Galois Connection and Widening / Narrowing Approaches to Abstract Interpretation. Symposium on Programming Language Implementation and Logic Programming.

[11] Cousot P. 1996. Abstract Interpretation. ACM Computing Surveys.

[12] Cousot P., Cousot R., 2001. Abstract Interpretation Based Formal Methods and Future Challenges. Informatics. 10 Years Back. 10 Years Ahead,.

[13] Deutsch A. 2003. Static Verification of Dynamic Properties. SIGAda.

[14] Regehr, J., Reid, A., Webb, K. 2003. Eliminating stack overflow by abstract interpretation. In Proc. of the 3rd International Conf. on Embedded Software (EMSOFT).

[15] DAEDALUS. 2011. http://www.di.ens.fr/~cousot/projects/DAEDALUS.

[16] Spoto A. 1982. JULIA: A Generic Static Analyser for the Java Bytecode.

[17] Polyspace. 2011. http://www.mathworks.com/products/polyspace.

# Making the Non-executable ACATS Tests Executable

Dan Eilers
Irvine Compiler Corp.
dan@irvine.com

Tero Koskinen
tero.koskinen@iki.fi

## ABSTRACT

The Ada Conformity Assessment Test Suite (ACATS) includes both positive and negative tests. The negative tests have intentional errors that a compiler is intended to diagnose with a compile-time error message. Interestingly, the negative tests also include numerous "OK" lines that the compiler must not reject. But the absence of an error message on the "OK" lines is not always a convincing demonstration that the "OK" lines were correctly compiled, since the negative tests are not executable. By removing the intentional errors from a copy of each negative test, we are able to compile and run the resulting modified tests, demonstrating more convincingly that the "OK" lines are correctly compiled.

## Categories and Subject Descriptors

D.2.4 [**Software Engineering**]: Software/Program Verification—*Validation*; D.3.4 [**Programming Languages**]: Processors—*Compilers*; D.3.2 [**Programming Languages**]: Language Classifications—*Ada*

## General Terms

Verification

## Keywords

ACATS, conformance, conformance testing, Ada, compiler, Ahven

## 1. INTRODUCTION

It is important that Ada compilers work correctly, or as least as close to correctly as is feasible. Ada is often used for high-integrity applications where the compiled code must be correct. Even when great effort is expended to prove that the source code is correct, what matters most is the correctness of the compiler-generated object code. Ada is also used for large-scale applications, where it can be disruptive to update the compiler to fix compiler errors. And Ada projects often use multiple compilers, or multiple versions of the same compiler, often over a long project lifetime, where it is highly desirable that the various compilers behave consistently.

Although there are various means of guarding against compiler errors, including testing and analysis (manual or automated) of the application's object code, perhaps the first line of defense is compiler assessment. IEC 61508-3:2010 chapter 7.4.4.4 [2] states "An assessment shall be carried out ... to determine ... the potential failure mechanisms of the tools that may affect the executable software. ..."

The Ada Conformity Assessment Test Suite (ACATS) [1] is a publicly available test suite intended to check Ada compilers for conformance with the Ada standard [3]. It is derived from the original Ada Compiler Validation Capability (ACVC) sponsored by DARPA [4], USAF, DISA [5], and the former Ada Joint Program Office (AJPO). ACATS includes both "positive" and "negative" tests. That is, tests that are intended to compile and run successfully, and those with errors that are intended to be rejected by the compiler.

ACATS testing ensures that all of the positive tests execute correctly, and all of the errors in the negative tests are correctly diagnosed. However, an important but perhaps less well understood aspect of ACATS consists of a substantial number of lines marked "-- OK", (or in a few cases, "-- O.K." or "--OK") interspersed among the intentional errors in the negative (also known as class B) tests. There are nearly 5000 of these "OK" lines and approximately 13500 intentional errors. On average, there are about three "OK" lines in each negative test program.

A compiler is expected to reject all the intentional errors without rejecting any of the "OK" lines. Generally, the "OK" lines are similar to the erroneous lines, effectively marking the boundary between what is legal and what is not. Sometimes they are actually identical, with the context determining legality as the result of visibility rules. One might assume that if these "OK" lines are important, they would also be included in some positive test, thereby demonstrating that they compile and execute correctly. But there does not appear to have been a systematic effort to do so. Instead, some "OK" lines are tested only to the extent that they are not rejected when mixed with intentional errors. We think this leaves room for improvement, as explained following.

Once a compiler detects an error, it may behave differently than before. In particular, it may abort any further involvement of the semantic analysis, code-generation, and optimization phases of the compiler. It also may restrict its error reporting, in an attempt to avoid redundant "cascad-


*SIGAda'11*, November 6–10, 2011, Denver, Colorado, USA.

ing" error messages resulting from the earlier error. Similarly, it may suppress reporting that an internal consistency check has failed, or that an internal exception was raised, on the assumption (perhaps sometimes overly optimistic) that the previous error was to blame.

So in order to adequately ensure that an "OK" line is compilable, one really needs to compile and run it in the context of a legal program. We accomplish this by modifying a copy of each ACATS negative test to remove the intentional errors. We also make any necessary additional modifications, such as providing initial values for otherwise uninitialized variables. This allows one to verify that the "OK" lines successfully compile and run normally, that is, without raising an exception or getting deadlocked or into an infinite loop. The result is a more credible means of demonstrating that a compiler actually satisfies all of the intended ACATS test objectives.

Section 2 describes the background of "OK" lines; section 3 describes the motivation for our work; section 4 describes related work identifying inadequately tested test objectives; section 5 describes our method; section 6 describes our results; and section 7 gives the conclusions.

## 2. BACKGROUND

All versions of ACVC and ACATS have used "OK" lines in negative tests. The original ACVC was developed according to detailed guidelines specified in the "Ada Compiler Validation Implementers' Guide" (IG) [6], and further explained in an accompanying paper, "The Ada Compiler Validation Capability" [7]. Considering how numerous the "OK" lines are, it is perhaps surprising that neither the IG nor the accompanying paper discusses the purpose or guidelines for the use of "OK" lines. There are however a few examples in the IG, particularly involving visibility rules in chapter 7, that do show both legal and illegal Ada constructs in the same program. Such examples could perhaps be construed as templates to be followed by the test writers. The ACATS Users' Guide [8] briefly mentions "OK" lines, but only to the extent that a compiler must not reject them (which is generally true of unmarked lines as well).

Perhaps even more surprising, considering that the ACVC and ACATS are segregated into positive and negative tests, is that the IG's test objectives are not similarly segregated. For example, in IG section 3.5.1, Test Objective 1 states: "Check that only identifiers and character literals (not string literals) are allowed as enumeration literals." This would appear to call for both a positive test (for identifiers and character literals), and a negative test (for string literals). What we find instead is a negative test, b35101a, that uses an "OK" line for the case of identifiers and character literals:

```
TYPE E1 IS (A, B, C, 'A', 'C', 'B');  -- OK.
TYPE E3 IS ("+", A);                  -- ERROR: "+".
```

There is no corresponding positive test that specifically tests the objective that identifiers and character literals are allowed in enumerations. But that turns out not to be a concern, because there are several positive tests that include identifiers and character literals in enumerations, specifically c34001a, c34001c, c35102a, c35504a, c35505c, c35507i, c35507j, c35507m, and c35507n. So this particular test objective is well covered, (no doubt intentionally) although the positive and negative tests are not cross-referenced to demonstrate that fact–neither in this specific case nor in general.

## 3. MOTIVATION

> People who analyze algorithms have double happiness. *Donald Knuth* [9]

Our recent personal experiences porting Ahven and other applications between various Ada compilers demonstrates that those compilers have some remaining errors of the kind that ACATS is intended to detect, even involving the older and presumably more well-exercised language features. The errors have come in all varieties, including rejecting legal programs, accepting illegal programs, failing to apply language-defined checks, generating incorrect code, and errors in the run-time system. In some cases, it was much easier to find the errors by simply porting the code and comparing the results, rather than by analysis or testing of the generated object code. So we are motivated to find ways to improve the effectiveness of ACATS, taking advantage of modern levels of available computing power, rather than being constrained by previous concerns over the test suite's size.

In the 1980's, running the ACVC was quite burdensome, due to its size and the relative slowness of available computers. Consequently, concerns were expressed that the ACVC should not get much larger. In fact, during the development of the Ada95 version of the ACVC, some low-value Ada83 ACVC tests were removed in order to keep the overall test suite to a manageable size. However, after about three decades of Moore's law, and the availability of multi-core processors, compiler testing today is hundreds or thousands of times faster than in the 1980's. So running ACATS is no longer burdensome, and increasing the size of the test suite is feasible.

A previous paper [10] showed how ACATS could be used by end-users in an unconventional way, to actually find errors in compilers that pass 100% of ACATS tests when run normally. The idea was to combine all the ACATS executable tests into a single program, using the Ahven testing framework to control the execution and summarize the test results. Ahven [11] is an open-source unit-testing framework for Ada, inspired by the JUnit testing framework for Java, with some ideas from AUnit.

Similarly, in this paper we describe another unconventional way for end-users to potentially find further compiler errors using ACATS, by executing the otherwise non-executable negative tests. The newly executable tests can be run along with the normal executable tests using the Ahven testing framework to do the grading and summarization, if desired, for double happiness.

Removing the error lines from the negative tests was suggested to us by Eachus [12] as a possibly worthwhile way to improve the effectiveness of ACATS. We found this suggestion particularly attractive, since it improves the effectiveness of ACATS with regard to its pre-existing test objectives, rather than requiring development of additional test objectives.

## 4. RELATED WORK

In 2007, during the development of the Ada 2005 version of ACATS, Randy Brukardt developed a partial cross reference [13] between the Ada Reference Manual and existing

ACATS tests in order to assess the coverage and need for additional tests. Specifically, it covers RM 3.9.3–3.10, RM 4.1.3–4.4, RM 6.5–6.7, RM 7.4–7.6.1, RM 8.3.1–8.5, and RM 10. He found at least the following cases where "OK" lines in negative tests were not adequately tested in positive tests:

Test: b393005
Objective: Check that a non-abstract function with a controlling result of type T is inherited as non-abstract and does not require overriding for a null extension of T.
Randy's comment: Note: this is tested (one example) in B393005, but no attempt is made to see if the result works.

Test: b431001
Objective: Check that the reference L.R can be interpreted as a prefixed view if the designator R represents a component of the type T that is not visible at the point of the reference.

Test: b831001
Objectives: Check that an overriding indicator can be given on an abstract subprogram declaration, a null procedure declaration, and an ordinary (non-protected) subprogram declaration.
Check that an overriding indicator can be given on a subprogram body, subprogram body stub, and a subprogram renaming declaration.
Check that an overriding indicator can be given on a generic instantiation of a subprogram.

Test: ba11014
Objectives: Check that nested packages are present in the limited view of a package. 10.1.1(12.2/2).
Check that all types are present in the limited view of a package, and all types are incomplete, and that tagged types are tagged incomplete. 10.1.1(12.3/2).
Randy's comment: ... other C-Tests will provide executable examples of some of the cases.

Tests: ba21002, ba21a02
Objective: Check that the elaboration of a preelaborated unit can include a call to a static function.
Randy's comment: Need some executable tests with these pragmas (not just occurrences in B-Tests).

Test: ba21a02
Objective: Check that the elaboration of a preelaborated unit can include the name of an enclosing type's discriminant.
Randy's comment: BA21001 claims to test this, but the expression is not evaluated when the type is elaborated and the type is not otherwise used, so it is bogus.

Randy points out in connection with b393005 that "no attempt is made to see if the result works." We note that by removing the "Error" lines from negative tests, we are demonstrating that the resulting tests compile and run normally, but we may still come short of demonstrating that the language feature actually "works" in the sense of producing a correct result. This leaves room for future work.

# 5. METHOD

It turns out that removing error lines is not as simple as first thought. The first obstacle to overcome is the sheer number of errors to remove, approximately 13500.

## 5.1 Removing error lines

Most of the errors to be removed consist of a single line that is straightforward to remove using an automated tool that deletes lines containing the pattern "-- ERROR:". For example:

```
I__2 := 2;    -- ERROR: CONSECUTIVE UNDERSCORES.
```

Sometimes the illegal construct spans multiple source lines, although in such cases, only one of the lines is marked, such as:

```
TYPE TERR4 IS DELTA 2#10#                 -- ERROR: 10
                   RANGE 2#0.0# .. 2#10.0#;
```

So deleting just the error line doesn't always work. Nor is it always possible to simply delete up to the next semicolon, in cases such as:

```
PROCEDURE TEST_OUT(I : OUT INTEGER := 12) IS  -- ERROR:
     BEGIN
          I := 12;
     END;
```

Normally, a single declaration or statement is either OK or not, but there are some unusual cases, such as:

```
O_6 : BA12015p.T_Data            -- OK.
          := BA12015p.Datum;     -- ERROR: Not visible.
```

and

```
PROCEDURE B37106A IS
   TYPE REC2 (DISC1 : DAY;           -- OK.
          DISC2 : DAY RANGE MON .. FRI) IS  -- ERROR:
                                  -- RANGE CONSTRAINT.
          RECORD
               NULL;
          END RECORD;
```

In one unusual case, the parameter name was used to indicate "OK", rather than a comment.

```
entry Naughty (Ok  : in Some_Type;
               Bad : access Some_Type);      -- ERROR:
```

In multi-line cases, the marked line is not always first. For example:

```
procedure Primitive_Of_Both_Proc1
          (P1 : Tagged_Of_Pk1_U;
           P2 : Tagged_Of_Pk1_S);             -- ERROR:
```

The multi-line cases can usually be found by compiling the code after deleting the single error lines, since deleting part of a declaration or statement will usually result in a compile-time error.

However, this isn't always true. For example, in the following anomalous case, deleting the two marked lines leaves a compilable program, but not what the test writer intended.

```
function BA11002_0.BA11002_2 (Int : Visible_Integer)
  return Private_Integer;                              -- ERROR:

function BA11002_0.BA11002_3 (Int : Private_Integer)   -- ERROR:
  return Visible_Integer;
```

Our intention with regard to multi-line errors is to add a distinct marker to the original source files to indicate the additional lines that would need to be removed when automatically removing the error lines. The existing error marker clearly can't be used for this purpose, because doing would interfere with tools used to grade B-test compile logs.

## 5.2 Making the tests legal

After deleting the errors, we are not always left with legal programs. Sometimes we are left with an empty subprogram, or an empty sequence-of-statements in a branch of an if-then-else statement, or a record-type declaration with no fields, or a function with no return statement, etc, and in such cases some straightforward cleanup, such as insertion of null statements, is required.

In most cases it would be harmless to add such new null statements to the original tests, although null record fields are somewhat problematic because a null field may not be combined with other fields.

## 5.3 Linking the tests

In some tests there are package or subunit specifications with no body provided, as confidently noted in this test comment:

```
-- Note: We don't provide a body for
-- B7310016_1.Places.P.R, as it shouldn't compile anyway.
```

So a number of package and subunit bodies had to be added in order to allow the tests to be linked and executed.

Some B-tests are in the form of one or more top-level packages, with no main procedure. In those cases, we added a main procedure, ensuring that each test has a main procedure, and each compilation unit is with'd, directly or indirectly, by the main procedure. In tests involving private child units, where it is not legal for the main procedure to directly depend on such a unit, additional package bodies were added as necessary.

In tests involving top-level generic packages, we added corresponding generic instantiations to the main programs, in order to better exercise the compiler.

## 5.4 Making the tests run normally

After getting the tests to compile cleanly, there was additional work needed to make the tests run normally, as discussed following.

In some cases, initial values needed to be provided for variables, such as Acc_To_New_Tag_Obj in B3A2002, GAT0 in B3A2004_0, Derf_L0 in B3A2012_0, Derf_L1 in B3A2012, A,B,D,E,G,H,J,K in B45501A, OBJ2,OBJ3,OBJ4 in B49004A, B in B49010A, A,C in B54A12A, CHAR,ENUM in B54B02B, X in B74207A, Int in B954003, Client_Var4 in BA12007_6, field Parent_Record.VI in BA11007_3, and Obj,Ptr in BDE0010.

In b455002, we needed to reinitialize variable F, in order to avoid a Constraint_Error resulting from overflow.

Many tests that include tasks had to be modified to match up entry calls with accept statements in order to avoid calling an entry of a completed task, or to avoid task deadlock, etc.

In some cases, array bounds needed to be adjusted to avoid raising Constraint_Error, including variable S in B34001B, S in B34001E, S in B34002B, concatenation results in B34005B,E,H,K, and ACC_STRING in B37101A.

In b330001, Constraint_Error was avoided by changing the discriminant for Constraint_Rec_Var from 4 to 3, and for Uncons_Tag_Var_W_Int from 1 to 3.

In B7310016_1.Places.P.Q, infinite recursion in A_Func_1 and A_Func_2 needed to be avoided.

Sometimes when a test was raising Constraint_Error, it wasn't obvious whether to try to prevent the error, such as by changing array bounds, or to add an exception handler to handle the error. We did some of each, on a somewhat ad hoc basis.

# 6. RESULTS

As a result of modifying and running the tests, we made various observations:

## 6.1 Errors found in tests

In two cases, Constraint_Error was raised at run time, indicating what appear to be unintentional errors in the original tests.

In b433001, we find:

```
type Test_Array_2 is array
   (Character range <>, Boolean range <>) of Rec;
O15: Test_Array_2('c'..'e',Boolean) :=
   ((Rec_1, Rec_2, Rec_3), (Rec_3, Rec_2, Rec_1)); -- OK.
O17: Test_Array_2('x'..'z',Boolean) :=
   ((Rec_1, Rec_2, Rec_3), (others => <>));         -- OK.
```

Both O15 and O17 are 3x2 arrays initialized with a 2x3 aggregate. Surprisingly, considering Ada's reputation for early detection of errors, this dimension mismatch is not illegal. Instead it results in Constraint_Error always being raised at run time.

In b960001, we find:

```
delay until ( Ada.Calendar.Time_Of (
                    Current_Year,
                    Current_Month,
                    Current_Year,
                    Current_Seconds) );   -- O.K.
```

It appears that Current_Day was intended in place of the second Current_Year. This is not illegal because Day_Number and Year_Number in package Ada.Calendar are both integer subranges rather than distinct types. But a year of 2011 passed as a parameter to a subprogram that is expecting a day in the range of 0..31 will always raise Constraint_Error at run time.

## 6.2 Other cases of deferred detection of errors

Early detection of errors was considered to be a "Study Topic", S2.3-A(1), in the requirements document for Ada95, so not a hard and fast requirement. Still, it can be somewhat surprising when Ada doesn't uphold this principle. Besides the previous two cases where detection of errors was deferred from compile-time to run-time, we also found similar cases that inevitably raise Constraint_Error at runtime, but a compiler must not reject them.

In b490001, we find:

```
type My_Int is range -128 .. 127;
subtype My_Int_Sub is My_Int range -100 .. 100;
SubInt1 : constant My_Int_Sub := -128;          -- OK.
     -- But raises Constraint_Error at run-time.
```

In b95031a we find:

```
TYPE NI3 IS NEW INTEGER RANGE 0..2;
TASK TYPE TT2 IS
     ENTRY E1 (NI3);
END TT2;
OBJ_TT2_2 : TT2;

OBJ_TT2_2.E1 (3);           -- OK.
    -- But 3 not in 0..2
```

In b460004, we find:

```
type Tag_Type is tagged record
   C1 : Natural := 5;
end record;

type DTag_Type is new Tag_Type with record
   C2 : String (1 .. 5) := "Hello";
end record;

Tag_Type_Operand : B460004_0.Tag_Type;
DTag_Type_Target : B460004_0.DTag_Type;

DTag_Type_Target := B460004_0.DTag_Type
  (B460004_0.Tag_Type'Class(Tag_Type_Operand)); -- OK.
```

These type conversions on the "OK" line inevitably raise Constraint_Error at run time.

In b85004a, we find package GENPKG instantiated before its body is seen, inevitably causing an elaboration-order violation at run-time.

In b85012a and b85015a, we find a subprogram renamed before its body is seen, inevitably causing elaboration-order violations at run-time.

In b92001a, we find:

```
POINTER_TT1_1 : ATT1 := NEW TT1;
POINTER_TT1_2 : ATT1 := NEW TT1;
POINTER_TT2_1 : ATT2 := NEW TT2;
```

These declarations allocate tasks before the task body is seen, which inevitably causes run-time errors.

## 6.3 Needed positive tests

As a result of finding various compiler problems, we have found a need for some additional positive tests. For example, there is apparently no positive test for overflow of fixed-point multiplication, although there is a test, c45523a, for overflow of floating-point multiplication, and there is a negative test, b455002, that when converted to a positive test causes overflow of multiplication between a fixed-point type and an integer.

Similarly, there is apparently no positive test corresponding to test bc51007 that demonstrates that Constraint_Error is raised when deriving one record type from another, where the records have discriminants of differing subtypes, and one of the subtype constraints is violated.

## 6.4 Observation regarding missing package body

In b392001, there is a missing package body. When we tried to add one, we found we couldn't! The following simplified version illustrates how a package body can be needed, but impossible to supply.

```
package P is
   type T1 is tagged null record;
   function Foo return T1;
   procedure Proc1 (x: T1'class := Foo);
   type T2 is new T1 with null record;
   function Foo return T2;
end P;

package body P is
   function Foo return T1 is
     begin return r: T1; end Foo;
   function Foo return T2 is
     begin return r: T2; end Foo;
   procedure Proc1 (x: T1'class := Foo) is
                       -- illegal, Foo is ambiguous
     begin null; end;
-- procedure Proc1 (x: T1'class := T1'(Foo)) is
--                     -- also illegal,
--   begin null; end;  -- default expression mismatch
end P;
```

# 7. CONCLUSIONS

We have succeeded in creating executable tests (that run normally) out of the ACATS non-executable tests. In doing so, we have noted various interesting things about the test suite, and about the Ada language itself. The resulting executable negative tests can be combined with the positive tests to create a single self-checking executable program using the Ahven testing framework. This large but easily built program can be used by Ada projects to easily assess an Ada compiler more comprehensively than using the conventional ACATS procedures. In particular, the nearly 5000 test objectives implemented by "OK" lines in negative tests are now compiled in the context of an executable program, that demonstrates more convincingly that they are correctly compiled.

*Acknowledgments.*

The authors would like to thank the anonymous referees for their helpful comments.

# 8. REFERENCES


[1] Randall L. Brukardt, "Ada Conformity Assessment Test Suite (ACATS)," http://www.ada-auth.org/acats.html.

[2] IEC 61508-3:2010 Functional safety of electrical/electronic/programmable electronic safety-related systems, Part 3: Software requirements, 2010.

[3] S. Tucker Taft, Robert A. Duff, Randall L. Brukardt, Erhard Ploedereder, Pascal Leroy, (Eds.) Ada 2005 Reference Manual. Language and Standard Libraries. International Standard ISO/IEC 8652/1995(E) with Technical Corrigendum 1 and Amendment 1, Lecture Notes in Computer Science, Vol. 4348, Springer, 2006.

[4] DARPA contract for Ada83 ACVC development, MDA903-79-C-0687, 1979.

[5] DISA contract for Ada95 ACVC development DCA100-97-D-0025.

[6] Ada Compiler Validation Implementers' Guide, SofTech, Waltham, Massachusetts, October, 1980.

[7] John B. Goodenough, "The Ada Compiler Validation Capability," *Computer*, vol. 13, no. 6, pp. 57-64, June 1981, doi:10.1109/C-M.1981.220496.

[8] Randall L. Brukardt, Ada Conformity Assessment Test Suite (ACATS) User's Guide, Version 3.0, 2008, http://www.ada-auth.org/acats-files/3.0/docs/ACATS-UG.PDF.

[9] Donald E. Knuth, Preface to Selected Papers on Analysis of Algorithms, Stanford, California: Center for the Study of Language and Information, 2000.

[10] Dan Eilers and Tero Koskinen, Adapting ACATS to the Ahven Testing Framework, Reliable Software Technologies – Ada-Europe 2011, Lecture Notes in Computer Science, 2011, Vol. 6652/2011, pp. 75-88.

[11] Tero Koskinen, Ahven developer, http://sourceforge.net/projects/ahven.

[12] Robert Eachus, Personal communication, May 2010.

[13] Randall L. Brukardt, ACATS 3.0 Test Objectives (partial), 2007. http://www.ada-auth.org/acats-files/3.0/devs/TESTOBJ.ZIP

# Language Choice for Safety Critical Applications

Jim Rogers
MEI Technologies, Inc.
2525 Bay Area Blvd., Suite 300
Houston, TX 77058
888-895-3014
James.Rogers@meitechinc.com

## ABSTRACT

The programming languages currently most popular among software engineers for writing safety critical applications are C and, more recently, C++. The Ada language has been designed with software safety in mind. Although Ada is not perfect concerning safety critical programming, it is far better than C or C++. There have been definitions of subsets of C for safety critical applications, such as MISRA C. Similarly, there are several attempts at defining a safe subset of C++, including MISRA C++ and the Joint Strike Fighter (JSF) Avionics C++ coding standards. The most commonly used safety critical subset of Ada is SPARK. SPARK provides a statically provable fully deterministic subset of Ada. The C and C++ safety critical subsets attempt to achieve a level of safety similar to the full Ada language. That attempt generally fails. This paper concentrates on a comparing the C++ language, including portions of the JSF C++ standard and those features inherited from C, with the full Ada language.

## Categories and Subject Descriptors

D.2.3 [**SOFTWARE ENGINEERING**]: Coding Tools and Techniques – *standards*

## General Terms

*Standardization, Languages*

## 1 OVERVIEW OF SOFTWARE SAFETY

Software safety is a specialization of System Safety. A software safety engineer is responsible for the safety of a system with a special focus on the role of software in the system.

Many engineers developing real-time and embedded software talk about safety-critical software, with the assumption that a system may be composed of both safety-critical and non-safety-critical software. The primary motivation behind this distinction is cost. Most of the safety-critical software development standards, such as DO-178B and ISO/IEC 12207, compartmentalize requirements so that systems with more risk are required to exhibit greater rigor in their development processes.

A software safety engineer must evaluate system requirements, along with mission requirements and system concepts of operation, to identify hazards related to the use of software. Some software-related hazards are the result of poor requirements. Some hazards are the result of incorrect software design. Some hazards are the result of hardware failures, such as radiation effects on computer memory. Some software-related hazards occur when software is used to correct for hardware failures, such as in system or subsystem fault detection, isolation, and recovery. It is also true that safety-critical software sharing hardware resources with non-safety-critical software can be affected by failures in the non-safety-critical software. For this reason the NASA software safety standard NASA-STD-8719.13 defines safety-critical software as

*4.1.1.2 Software shall be classified as safety-critical if it meets at least one of the following criteria:*

*a. Resides in a safety-critical system (as determined by a hazard analysis) AND at least one of the following apply:*

*1) Causes or contributes to a hazard.*

*2) Provides control or mitigation for hazards.*

*3) Controls safety-critical functions.*

*4) Processes safety-critical commands or data (see note 4-1 below).*

*5) Detects and reports, or takes corrective action, if the system reaches a specific hazardous state.*

*6) Mitigates damage if a hazard occurs.*

*7) Resides on the same system (processor) as safety-critical software (see note 4-2 below).*


*SIGAda'11*, November 6–10, 2011, Denver, Colorado, USA.

*b. Processes data or analyzes trends that lead directly to safety decisions (e.g., determining when to turn power off to a wind tunnel to prevent system destruction).*

*c. Provides full or partial verification or validation of safety-critical systems, including hardware or software subsystems.*

*Note 4-1: If data is used to make safety decisions (either by a human or the system), then the data is safety-critical, as is all the software that acquires, processes, and transmits the data. However, data that may provide safety information but is not required for safety or hazard control (such as engineering telemetry) is not safety-critical.*

*Note 4-2: Non-safety-critical software residing with safety-critical software is a concern because it may fail in such a way as to disable or impair the functioning of the safety-critical software. Methods to separate the code, such as partitioning, can be used to limit the software defined as safety-critical. If such methods are used, then the isolation method is safety-critical, but the isolated non-critical code is not.*

While it is well understood that software correctness, particularly when the software is developed using a large team of people, is significantly enhanced by the adoption of rigorous development processes, it is also true that processes alone will not result in correct software. Other critically important factors in software development include the experience and training of the software development team, the schedule allowed for development, the funding available for development, and the tools used to accomplish the development effort.

This paper focuses on one kind of tool used for software development; the programming language. Many papers have been written asserting that the choice of programming language is inconsequential to the overall result. Many engineering management teams have accepted these assertions as truth and use this so-called "truth" to justify choosing the tools supported by the least expensive labor force. In the world of safety-critical programming the languages supported by the least expensive labor force have, for many years, been C and C++. There is a glut of C and C++ programmers in the world of software development. They pour out of colleges, universities, and technical schools like a mighty river. Unfortunately, use of the C and C++ languages results in significant hidden costs and safety risks due to the clumsiness and lack of precision the languages provide as safety-critical programming tools.

## 1.1 Comparison of Ada and C++ for use in safety-critical software

Ada was designed from the start to support development of safety-critical real-time systems. C++ was designed to be an object-oriented extension of the C language. The C language was designed to be a high level assembly language used to develop the Unix operating system.

## 1.2 C++ is largely a superset of C

C++ syntax comes from C syntax. The languages are close enough that most C programs will compile correctly on a C++ compiler without modification of the original C program

**Table 1 C++ Language features**

| Language Feature | Inherited from C | New to C++ |
|---|---|---|
| **Syntax** | X | X (extends) |
| **Arrays (no range checking)** | X | |
| **Numeric types** | X | |
| **Permitting incomplete forward declarations** | X | |
| **Public, private, protected scoping** | | X |
| **Type casting** | X | X(extends) |
| **Struct** | X | X(extends) |
| **Class** | | X |
| **Union** | X | X(extends) |
| **Generic programming** | | X |
| **Pointers** | X | |
| **References** | | X |
| **Const** | | X |
| **Namespaces** | | X |
| **Pre-processor** | X | |
| **Boolean type** | | X |
| **Numeric type upper and lower limits defined in header files** | X | |
| **Numeric overflow not detected** | X | |
| **Switch statement syntax** | X | |
| **Strings** | X | |

Hello World in C++:

```
#include <iostream>

int main()
{
 std::cout << "Hello, World." <<
std::endl;
}
```

## 2 C++ TYPE SYSTEM

Numeric types have ranges based upon hardware layout rather than upon application requirements. Recompiling a C++ program from a 32 bit processor to a 64 bit processor will change the ranges of all numeric types. On the 32 bit machine an int will occupy 32 bits, while it will occupy 64 bits on a 64 bit machine. Assumptions about the valid range of values for an int are unwise. C++ reports the size of its data types in units of bytes, which are assumed to be 8 bits in length. Thus, on a 32 bit machine the size of an int is 4, while on a 64 bit machine the size of an int will be 8.

There are normally three different signed integer types defined in C++: short, int, long. The official rule for those types states that a short is no longer than an int, and an int is no longer than a long. It is allowed for all three types to have the same length.

Pointers contain hardware addresses. They are stored in the form of an integer, and there is a peculiar form of integer mathematics for pointers. One can assign values to pointers, compare pointers, and add integer values to or subtract integer values to from pointers. Adding 1 to a pointer does not result in an address pointing to the next bit in memory. If a pointer is defined as an int pointer, then adding 1 to the pointer results in the memory address of what is assumed to be the next non-overlapping int in memory. If an int is 32 bits, or 4 bytes, long, then adding 1 to an int pointer will advance the address contained in the pointer by 4 bytes. Pointer arithmetic was introduced in C, and carried over to C++, for the purpose of manipulating arrays.

In C and C++ the name of an array is defined as a pointer to the first element in the array. Adding 1 to that pointer results in the address of the 2nd element in the array, and so forth. Since C and C++ provide no automatic array bounds checking, one can use pointer arithmetic to point anywhere in memory. Array indices in C and C++ are a short hand for pointer arithmetic. The index value indicates the number of elements beyond the first element. Every C or C++ array index begins at 0, since that indicates the address of the start of the array plus 0 elements.

**Table 2 C++ Array Syntax**

```
int values[10];//Declare an array of 10 ints
values[0] = 1; //Assigning 1 to the first
               // element
values[1] = 2; //Assigning 2 to the second
               //element
values[9] = 10; //Assigning 10 to the 10th
                //element
```

## 2.1 C++ array syntax safety concerns

- Array indexing is always off by one from the array element number, resulting in a tendency to index one past the end of an array.
- Since an array name is no more than a pointer to the first element of the array, C++ array syntax provides no array bounds checking.
- Every array must be indexed using integers.
- There is no way to specify the index type for an array.
- Every array index must begin at 0.
- C++ array syntax requires software developers to map the problem space to the hardware-based representation of the array, resulting in algorithmic complexity.
- Two-dimensional arrays are often indexed by a single index using a combination of multiplication and division. This maps closely to memory but does not support the concept of a matrix in a clear and unambiguous manner.
- C++ array bounds must be explicitly programmed every time the array is traversed, making maintenance of arrays error prone.
- Bounds checking of array indices must be manually programmed, and is often overlooked in C++ programs.

**Table 3 Multi-dimensional array in C++**

```
int mat1[10][10]; //declaration of a matrix
int mat2[100]; //declaration of a matrix
mat1[2][0] = 9; //Assign 9 to 1st element of
                //row 3
mat2[(10 * 2) + 0] = 9; //Same as above

int i, j;
for(i = 0; i < 10; i++)
          {
          for(j = 0; j < 10; j++)
                 mat1[i][j] = 0;
          } //Assigning 0 to all array
            //elements
```

## 2.2 Ada array syntax

Ada array declarations include the declaration of the index type and the element type. All array access operations are protected by bounds checking of the array. Ada array indices may be of any discrete type.

**Table 4 Ada array syntax**

```
Subtype index_type is integer range
                                 1..10;
Type matrix is array(index_type,
                   index_type) of integer;
Mat1 : matrix;
Mat1(3,1) := 9;  -- Assign 9 to the 1st
                 -- element of row 3

For I in Mat1'Range(1) loop
   For J in Mat1'Range(2) loop
      Mat1(I,J) := 0;
   End loop;
End loop;
```

## 2.3 Ada syntax safety benefits

- Ada allows the array index values to be mapped to the problem domain
- Ada arrays are first class types, not merely side effects of pointer manipulation. This prevents unexpected results due to pointer complications
- Ada implicitly checks array bounds
- The Ada 'Range attribute maintains proper array bounds manipulation even when the index subtypes are changed due to maintenance.

# 3 STRINGS

## 3.1 C++ strings

C++ commonly uses C-style strings. C++ also provides a String class which is sometimes used. C-style strings are used for C++ string literals. A C-style string is an array of char terminated by a null character. Most C++ string handling functions start processing the string at the beginning of the array and continue processing until they encounter the null character. Failure to put a null character at the end of the useful data in a string will result in either garbage data or array bounds violations, which will not be caught by the language or the executing program.

String assignment merely copies pointer values, causing both strings to point to the same address in memory. To duplicate a string each element of the source string must be copied into the destination string.

**Table 5 C-style arrays**

```
char name[30];
char name2[10];
name = "Jim Rogers";
//uses 11 elements including
//the null character
strcpy(name2, name);
//copy name to name2
```

The strcpy function shown above copies the elements from name into name2, ending its processing upon processing the null character. The function strcpy assume that the destination string is large enough to contain all the elements copied from the source string. In the example above the 10 characters in "Jim Rogers" are copied from name into name2, and then the null character is copied in to the 11th character memory address following the start of the array name. A bounds violation occurs and memory outside the array is corrupted.

**Table 6 Using the strncpy function**

```
char name[30];
char name2[10];
name = "Jim Rogers";
strncpy(name2, name, 10);
//copy 10 characters from
//name to name2
```

The strncpy function takes a 3rd argument indicating the number of elements to copy from the source string to the destination string. Unfortunately, in this example, no null character is copied into name2. Subsequent processing of name2 will result in reading beyond the end of the array.

## 3.2 Safety concerns for C++ strings

C++ strings are somewhat similar to Ada bounded strings. Logically the information they contain may be any size up to the limit of the buffer reserved in memory to hold that string object. C++ strings, however, lack the safety of Ada bounded strings since they do not automatically maintain information about the logical length of the information contained in the string, nor do they prevent storage of information beyond the physical end of the string object.

The use of the null character as a meta-character to mark the end of a string is error-prone. When the null character is omitted from a string the C++ library routines, and most custom string handling routines, will process data beyond the end of the proper string information, and possibly beyond the array reserved for the string object.

The two standard functions for copying C++ strings are error prone due to the possibility of buffer overruns and the need to provide a null character at the end of the logical data in the string.

## 3.3 Ada string types

Ada provides 3 forms for strings. The String type is a fixed length string. The Unbounded_String type provides a fixed buffer that can contain string data up to the length of the buffer. The Unbounded_String type uses a dynamically allocated buffer to contain data without pre-defining the length. All three string types are safe to use. There is no need for special functions or procedures to copy on string to another, one unbounded_string to another, or one bounded_string to another.

## 3.4 Ada string benefits

Ada string manipulation cannot corrupt data outside the buffer reserved for the string.

# 4 C++ SWITCH STATEMENT

The C++ switch statement is the language's implementation of a case statement. It allows the program flow to jump to a label in the source code and continue execution at that point.

**Table 7 C++ Switch Statement**

```
switch ( expression )
      case constant-expression : statement
   [default  : statement]
```

```
switch (x) {
  case 1:
  case 2:
  case 3:
    cout << "x is 1, 2 or 3";
    break;
  default:
    cout << "x is not 1, 2 nor 3";
  }
```

Execution continues until the end of the compound block defined by the curly braces, or until a *break* statement is encountered. In the example above if x is 1, 2, or 3, the result will be an output stating "x is 1, 2, or 3". If x is any other value then the output following the "*default*" alternative will be executed. The break statement breaks out of the switch block. Failure to include the break statement will result in both output commands being executed if x is 1, 2, or 3. The C++ switch statement compares the value of *expression* with each case constant-expression. Each case constant-expression takes on the form of a label in the syntax, and it not executable. Upon finding an equality between the expression and a case constant-expression, execution begins at the first executable statement following the matching label. Note that C++ allows the use of floating point types in the case expression and in the case constant-expressions. Floating point equality comparisons are problematic, and their use is strongly discouraged.

## 4.1 Safety concerns with C++ switch statements

The default label is entirely optional in a C++ switch statement. It is not common practice for C++ programmers to use the default label. This is particularly true if the programmer is parsing through the values of an enumerated type. Programmers seldom consider that the number of enumeration values may be changed in the future. If they are, and no default label is used, the switch statement will not handle the additional values. There is no requirement in C++ for a switch statement to handle all values of the type in *expression*.

## 4.2 Ada case statement

The Ada case statement is defined for use only with discrete types. There is no possibility of using the case statement with any other kind of type.

**Table 8 Ada case statement**

```
case_statement ::=
  case expression is
    case_statement_alternative
    {case_statement_alternative}
  end case;

case_statement_alternative ::=
  when discrete_choice_list =>
   sequence_of_statements
```

```
case Bin_Number(Count) is
  when 1 => Update_Bin(1);
  when 2 => Update_Bin(2);
  when 3 | 4 =>
    Empty_Bin(1);
    Empty_Bin(2);
  when others => raise Error;
end case;
```

The sequence of statements executed after a matching case statement alternative is terminated either by encountering the "end case" clause, or by encountering another case statement alternative. Either the case statement must have a separate case statement alternative for every value of the type of *expression*, or the case statement must be terminated with an "*others*" alternative.

## 4.3 Ada case statement safety benefits

There is never a case when a new value is added to an enumerated type which is not handled in a case statement whose expression evaluates to that type. There is no chance of unintended fall-through due to the lack of a break statement.

# 5 ESTABLISHING FILE DEPENDENCIES

Every program must be able to establish dependencies between source file so that objects and methods defined in one source file may be called or referenced in another source file. C++ uses the same pre-processor technology found in the C language. Ada does not.

## 5.1 C++ pre-processor

The C++ pre-processor parses each source file before compilation. The pre-processor has its own syntax, separate from the C++ language. The primary role of the pre-processor is to copy source files from the designated source into the current source file. Thus, the text parsed by the C++ compiler is a combination of the source file as stored in your configuration management system and the contents of the files named in as *#include* files for the pre-processor. The pre-processor can also define constants and macros. Macros are bits of code expanded into the source file according to the syntax of the pre-processor.

**Table 9 C++ macros**

```
#define <identifier> <replacement token list>
#define <identifier>(<parameter list>) <replacement token list>
```

```
#define PI 3.14159
```

```
#define RADTODEG(x) ((x) * 57.29578)
```

In the first macro example above, the pre-processor scans the text of the current file looking for the token PI. Everywhere that token is found, it replaces the token with 3.14159. In the second macro the expansion is more function-like. Everywhere the pre-processor identified the token RADTODEG it removes the token and expands the parameter in parentheses to be ((parameter) * 57.29578). The parameter can be any identifier or literal. If the source code for a file contained both the macro definitions above, then the following substitutions are possible:

**Table 10 Macro expansion example**

| Code Before Substitution | Code After Substitution |
| --- | --- |
| RADTODEG(PI) | ((3.14159) * 57.29578) |

Pre-processor macros are also used to control conditional behavior of the pre-processor. It is an error to *#include* the same file more than once in each source file. This rule is complicated further because each file copied using a *#include* may *#include* other files. The end result would be multiple definition of the same constants and macros. It is common practice to place pre-processor macro and constant definitions in a *header* file. The *header* file name is commonly designated by ending in ".h". Inside the header files are "include directives" which prevent multiple inclusions of the same file in a single source file.

**Table 11 C++ include guard example**

| Filename | Pre-Processor syntax |
|---|---|
| grandfather.h | `#ifndef GRANDFATHER_H`<br>`#define GRANDFATHER_H`<br><br>`struct foo {`<br>`    int member;`<br>`};`<br>`#endif` |
| father.h | `#include "grandfather.h"` |
| child.c | `#include "grandfather.h"`<br>`#include "father.h"` |

Without the include guard the definition of "struct foo" from "grandfather.h" would be included twice, once directly, and once by including the file in "father.h".

## 5.2 Safety concerns with the C++ pre-processor

Pre-processor macros are not type-safe. The pre-processor has no knowledge of C++ syntax and does not know anything about the types of parameters substituted in macros. The programmer could easily pass any type, including a string or other compound type, in the place of the parameter, where a numeric value is expected. The result of such an error is undefined by the language. The use of pre-processor macros is generally discouraged for C++. . This problem is further compounded by the fact that C++ identifiers and keywords are case sensitive. It is common practice to name macro labels using all upper case. It is also common practice to name all constants within C++ source code using all upper case letters. It is common to see identifiers differing only in their use of upper and lower case, on the same line in a C++ program such as:

```
float pi = PI;
```

This mixture of very similar tokens within the source code is often problematic during code review of large bodies of source code.

Include guards are highly encouraged when programming in C++. Failure to use include guards will often result in multiple definitions of the same identifiers.

## 5.3 Ada context clause

Ada establishes file dependencies using the "*with*" clause. A "*with*" clause is also known as a "*context clause*". A context clause identifies separately compiled units needed by the current compilation unit. There is no modification of the current source file to include identifiers or tokens. The compiler performs the checks and scope definitions for each unit named in a context clause. The Ada language does definition does not include a pre-processor.

## 5.4 Safety advantages of the Ada context clause

What you see is what you get. There are no surprises due to textual inclusion or macro expansion. There are no facilities to create type-unsafe code through the improper expansion of a macro.

# 6 NUMERIC RANGE PROTECTION

## 6.1 C++ overflow, underflow, and range checking

C++ provides no built-in underflow or overflow protection. This protection can be written into classes, but must be manually coded by the programmer. Converting a numeric type to a class with overflow and underflow protection is both tedious and error-prone. More commonly, programmers find they need to provide a degree of range checking for C++. Range checking is also not provided by the language, and must be manually implemented. In many cases range checking is implemented as an afterthought, and not as a primary design requirement of the program.

The standard header file limits.h is commonly used to define upper and lower limits for C++ numeric types. Programmers may use the values in the limits.h file to predict underflow and overflow.

When a class is used to encapsulate all the range checking for a numeric type with a restricted range of valid values, the arithmetic operators for that class must be overridden to provide the appropriate range checking. Those overridden operators must subsequently be verified for correctness, which often is more expensive than writing the classes.

## 6.2 Safety concerns with C++ underflow, overflow, and range checking

The effort to provide overflow, underflow, or range checking in a C++ program is labor intensive and expensive. Both the software engineering staff and management are reticent to commit the resources necessary for proper overflow, underflow, and range checking of C++ programs. The result is often inadequate or non-existent overflow, underflow, or range checking.

### 6.3 Ada overflow, underflow, and range checking

Every Ada numeric type has a clearly defined lower limit and upper limit, which is known by the compiler. The attribute 'First contains the lower limit for the type. The attribute 'Last contains the upper limit for the type. The compiler produces and optimizes range checking code for all non-modular numeric types. Modular numeric types properly perform wrap-around within their specified range of values.

From the point of view of the Ada programmer, Ada range checking is specified when the lower and upper limits for a numeric type are defined. No expensive programming effort is required to provide range checking.

### 6.4 Safety advantages of Ada range checking

Range limits are easily specified as part of the definition of numeric types and subtypes. The ease of the effort encourages the use of numeric types and subtypes specialized for use in the application domain. The compiler writes and optimizes the actual range checking code as a default behavior. The result is a system with proper range checking throughout.

## 7 PARAMETER PASSING

### 7.1 C++ parameter passing

All parameters in C++ are passed by value. If the programmer wants to implement a pass by reference mechanism the programmer must pass a pointer or reference to the item. The pointer or reference is then passed by value. Since a C++ array name is a pointer to the first element of the array, there is no clear syntax distinguishing the passing of an array from the passing of a pointer to a scalar value. The programmer must assume that the parameter being passed is either an array, or is not. If an array is passed, then one must frequently also pass a second parameter indicating the size of the array. This requirement is not always followed for strings, since the C++ string data is processed from the address passed until a null character is encountered.

If a value is passed using a pointer or a reference, there is no syntax in C++ to indicate whether the value should or should not be changed within the called function.

### 7.2 Safety concerns with C++ parameter passing

Correct C++ function parameter passing relies heavily upon the knowledge or intuition of the programmer. Function comments must document the intention of the original programmer. Function comments are often wrong or out-dated, making them an unreliable control for proper parameter passing. Improper C++ function parameter passing can lead to unexpected side effects and buffer overflows.

### 7.3 Ada subprogram parameter passing

Every Ada subprogram parameter has an associated passing mode of either IN, OUT, or IN OUT. The compiler controls whether a parameter is passed by value or by reference.

### 7.4 Safety advantages of Ada parameter passing

Side effects of parameter passing are strictly controlled though language syntax, not merely by subprogram comments. Ada arrays cannot be confused with pointers to scalar objects, preventing any chance of buffer overflows. Ada arrays are passed with information about their size and the range of index values in the array, further preventing buffer overflows.

## 8 STATEMENTS

### 8.1 C++ statements

A statement in C++ can either be a simple statement or a compound statement. A simple statement is any single logical line of code ending with a semi-colon. A compound statement is 0 or more simple statements encapsulated in curly braces "{}". Simple statements and compound statements can be used interchangeably. The result is often logic errors due to program evolution or maintenance.

**Table 12 C++ statements example**

| Simple Statement | Compound Statement |
|---|---|
| `if (condition)`<br>`statement;` | `if (condition) {`<br>`    [statement]`<br>`}` |
| `if (a < b) c = 10;` | `if (a < b) {`<br>`    c = 10;`<br>`}` |
| `if (a < b) c = 10;`<br>`    return 0;` | `if (a < b){`<br>`    c = 10;`<br>`    return 0`<br>`}` |

In the examples above, the code in both columns in the middle row is fully equivalent, while the code in both columns in the third row is very different. In the column labeled "Simple Statement" the "return 0" will be executed whether "(a < b)" evaluates to true or false, while the code in the column labeled "Compound Statement" the "return 0" will only be executed if "(a < b)" evaluates to true. All the examples above are valid C++ code. No compiler diagnostics will be reported in any of the cases, but use of the simple statement, followed by adding another action, results in erroneous logic.

### 8.2 Safety concerns with C++ statements

C++ simple statements can result in erroneous logic as a program evolves or is maintained.

## 8.3 Ada statements

Ada provides full statement block structure and does not allow substitution of a simple statement where a block is required. For instance, Ada has no equivalent to the C++ examples in the column labeled "Simple Statement" above.

## 8.4 Safety advantages of Ada statements

The full block structure of Ada statements prevents future maintenance issues based upon programmer error due to confusion of simple and block statements.

# 9 GLOBAL ERROR HANDLING

## 9.1 C++ use of C libraries

Many C++ programs use C libraries. Most C libraries handle errors by setting a global variable named errno. This value is intended to hold the integer value corresponding to the latest error encountered during processing.

## 9.2 Safety concerns with global error handling

Global error handling does not support concurrent program design, including interrupt handling. In a concurrent program design the value of a global error location such as errno can be overwritten several times before it is read, causing the error handling routine to respond to the wrong error, or to miss one or more errors completely.

## 9.3 Ada global error handling

Ada does not provide a global error handling mechanism such as errno. Instead, errors are handled through the exception mechanism.

## 9.4 Safety advantages of Ada error handling

Ada error handling works properly with any degree of concurrency in the design.

# 10 BIT FIELD REPRESENTATIONS

## 10.1 C++ bit field representations

C++ allows the definition of bit fields to map memory layout to hardware or communication protocols. The C++ syntax for defining bit fields allows the programmer to specify the number of bits, but not the position of the fields. Each compiler may choose to lay out the bit fields in its own way.

**Table 13 C++ Bitfield**

```
// bit_fields1.cpp
struct Date
{
   unsigned nWeekDay  : 3;    // 0..7   (3 bits)
   unsigned nMonthDay : 6;    // 0..31  (6 bits)
   unsigned nMonth    : 5;    // 0..12  (5 bits)
   unsigned nYear     : 8;    // 0..100 (8 bits)
};

int main()
{
}
```

```
// bit_fields2.cpp
struct Date
{
   unsigned nWeekDay  : 3;    // 0..7   (3 bits)
   unsigned nMonthDay : 6;    // 0..31  (6 bits)
   unsigned           : 0;    // Force alignment
to next boundary.
   unsigned nMonth    : 5;    // 0..12  (5 bits)
   unsigned nYear     : 8;    // 0..100 (8 bits)
};

int main()
{
}
```

The first example specifies 21 bits, but does not specify memory alignment. The second example adds a new term with a length of 0, which forces alignment for the memory boundary of the next unsigned int.

In both cases the compiler is free to choose where to put the bit padding to fill out the memory alignment.

## 10.2 Safety concerns with C++ bit fields

Data alignment for standardized communication protocols can be error prone due to the lack of control the programmer has over the layout of the specified fields and the padding within a memory word.

There is also no language facility for determining word order of the layout. The word layout is compiler-specific.

## 10.3 Ada record representation clauses

Ada provides record representation clauses instead of bit fields. Record representation clauses provide much more control over the bit layout of the data and the range of valid values represented by that bit layout.

Table 14 Ada record representation clause

```
Word : constant := 4; -- storage element is
byte, 4 bytes per word

type State is (A,M,W,P);
type Mode  is (Fix, Dec, Exp, Signif);

type Byte_Mask  is array (0..7) of Boolean;
type State_Mask is array (State) of Boolean;
type Mode_Mask  is array (Mode) of Boolean;

type Program_Status_Word is
record
   System_Mask     : Byte_Mask;
   Protection_Key  : Integer range 0 .. 3;
   Machine_State   : State_Mask;
   Interrupt_Cause : Interruption_Code;
   Ilc             : Integer range 0 .. 3;
   Cc              : Integer range 0 .. 3;
   Program_Mask    : Mode_Mask;
   Inst_Address    : Address;
end record;

for Program_Status_Word use
record
   System_Mask     at 0*Word range  0 ..  7;
   Protection_Key  at 0*Word range 10 .. 11; --
bits 8,9 unused
   Machine_State   at 0*Word range 12 .. 15;
   Interrupt_Cause at 0*Word range 16 .. 31;
   Ilc             at 1*Word range  0 ..  1;  --
second word
   Cc              at 1*Word range  2 ..  3;
   Program_Mask    at 1*Word range  4 ..  7;
   Inst_Address    at 1*Word range  8 .. 31;
end record;

for Program_Status_Word'Size use
8*System.Storage_Unit;
for Program_Status_Word'Alignment use 8;
```

## 10.4 Safety advantages of Ada record representation clauses

Ada record representation clauses allow both the number of bits and the position within the set of words to be specified. This eliminates errors due to implementation-defined padding or ordering decisions made by a compiler.

# 11 TIMING

While C++ programmers commonly call the "sleep" function to delay program execution for some period of time, that function is not part of the C++ standard. Instead, it is part of library functions available on common Posix compliant operating systems. The commonly used sleep function takes an argument indicating the integer number of seconds to sleep. If you want to a finer granularity you must use the usleep function, which takes an integer argument for the number of microseconds to sleep. Other libraries provide versions of sleep that accept an integer number of microseconds as an argument.

## 11.1 Safety concerns with the C++ approach

Using operating system libraries, or other 3rd party libraries, to pause the execution of a program is only as portable as the library. For safety-critical systems all libraries used in safety-critical code must be certified for correctness. Addition of 3rd party libraries can greatly increase the certification costs of system using C++. Those extra costs frequently result in requests for waivers of certification requirements. While certification itself does not create safer code, the lack of certification leaves uncontrolled safety risks in a system.

## 11.2 Ada time and delay

The Ada.Calendar package defines a time type and forms of delays. The relative delay function takes an argument of type Duration, which is a pre-defined fixed-point type expressing a time in seconds. The implementation of Duration requires that the maximum time it can express is at least 86,400 seconds, and the minimum interval it can express cannot be more than 20 milliseconds. Implementation advice states that, whenever possible, the minimum interval for type Duration should not be more than 100 microseconds.

## 11.3 Safety advantages of Ada timing

The Ada delay and "delay until" subprograms are available on every Ada implementation. There is no added certification cost for their use. There are no requests for waivers of certification associated with their use.

# 12 FUNCTION RETURN VALUES

## 12.1 C++ functions return values can be ignored

C++ has only one kind of subprogram, the function. Every subprogram definition must define the type return by the function. It is possible, due to inheritance of syntax from C, for a C++ function definition to omit the name of its return type. In this case the compiler assumes the return type is "int". If you want a function to return nothing, then the specified return type is "void".

Whatever the return type of a function is, the program is allowed to ignore the returned value. Historically much C code used return values to indicate function success or failure. Many programmers simply ignore such status because their program designs assume everything works correctly all the time. C, and by inheritance, C++, allow programs to ignore function return values.

## 12.2 Safety concerns with ignoring C++ function return values

If the return value of a function is the primary operational output of the function, then ignoring the function return value always results in erroneous execution of a program. If the return value of a function is used to indicate success or failure of the function, then simply assuming success results in failure to detect program or system faults. One of the critical uses of software in safety-critical systems is the performance of Fault Detection, Isolation, and Response (FDIR). Any failure to detect, isolate, or respond to a system fault can result in serious or catastrophic failure of a safety-critical system.

## 12.3 Ada function return values cannot be ignored

Ada function return values can be used for the same purposes as C++ function return values. However, they cannot be ignored in the program. While this rule does not ensure that a program will handle return values properly, it does mean that they must be handled in some manner.

## 12.4 Safety advantages of handling Ada return values

Forcing programs to handle function return values aids the verification of correctness for programs. It also forces engineers to schedule some effort to deal with function return values instead of ignoring that effort in project planning.

# 13 CONCURRENCY

C++ provides no support for concurrency. Several 3rd party libraries exist for the implementation of concurrency in C++ programs. Some libraries, such as the pThreads library, are written in C, and do not support a clean interface between C++ classes and threads. Other libraries, such as the Boost thread libraries, provide a better C++ interface, but only encapsulate low level operating system capabilities in concurrency.

## 13.1 Safety concerns with C++ concurrency solutions

Full language support for concurrency requires subtle changes to the C++ memory model, understanding of timing, most importantly, syntax. Those syntax changes have been the primary reason the C++ language committee has chosen to leave C++ concurrency in the hands of external libraries. Without a full commitment to internal language support for concurrency one cannot assure that language features behave correctly in concurrent programs. For instance, how are exceptions handled across C++ threads? Are templates shared across threads, or are they local to each thread? How is memory shared between threads? How are threads scheduled? Which C++ libraries are safe to use in a concurrent program? Which are not? The C++ standard does not address any of these questions. Each program must be designed with its own solutions to these problems. The additional burden of complexity required for use of concurrency in C++ makes the whole issue daunting to C++ programmers.

All real-time safety-critical systems exhibit a mixture of sequential and concurrent behaviors. Inability to design effectively for such a mixture results in programs that have subtle but catastrophic failure modes.

## 13.2 Ada concurrency

Ada has always had the ability to define concurrent tasks and the interactions between those tasks. Each new version of the Ada standard has added features to the set of concurrency capabilities defined for the language. The 1995 standard added the most changes important to date with the addition of protected types and protected objects. Ada concurrency features such as tasks, task entries, protected types and objects, protected subprograms, requeue statements, and asynchronous abort statements, provide abstractions of concurrent behavior and control. Those abstractions reduce the complexity presented to the programmer and allow concurrency to be used without fear. There is still need for some concern over deadlocks, livelocks, and priority inversion issues, but Ada provides tools to deal with those issues.

## 13.3 Safety advantages of Ada concurrency

While Ada concurrency features provide continuing challenges to teams developing formal analysis tools for Ada, they are not in themselves unsafe. Concurrency requires a degree of asynchronous behavior in a program. That asynchronous behavior should only be used to model the problem domain, not as a goal of its own. Failure to properly accommodate the asynchronous nature of reality always eventually results in a safety problem. Tightly synchronized systems are relatively easier to verify and validate than are many asynchronous systems when one concentrates on the nominal behavior of a system. Human inputs, hardware failures, and environmental effects are always asynchronous. Ada provides the tools for dealing with those asynchronous events far better than does C++.

# 14 CONCLUSION

The choice of programming languages is important to the safety of modern safety-critical systems. The Ada language was designed to support the needs of safety-critical systems. The C++ language was not. People are currently trying to adapt C++ for use in safety-critical systems. The success of those efforts will be reported by others. Early data indicates that use of C++ is always more difficult and more expensive than indicated by initial project schedules and budgets, and the safety achieved by the use of C++ is at best adequate.

# 15 REFERENCES

National Aeronautics and Space Administration. (2004, July 8). Software Safety Standard. *NASA-STD 8719.13B* . Washington, DC, United States of America.

# Author Index

www.ingramcontent.com/pod-product-compliance
Lightning Source LLC
Chambersburg PA
CBHW081510200326
41518CB00015B/2447

* 9 7 8 1 4 5 0 3 1 4 0 0 8 *